Empowered:
The Baptism in the Holy Spirit

Alistair J Matheson

Copyright © 2023 Alistair Matheson

All rights reserved.

ISBN: 9798394614286

Dedicated to Peter Nicolson.

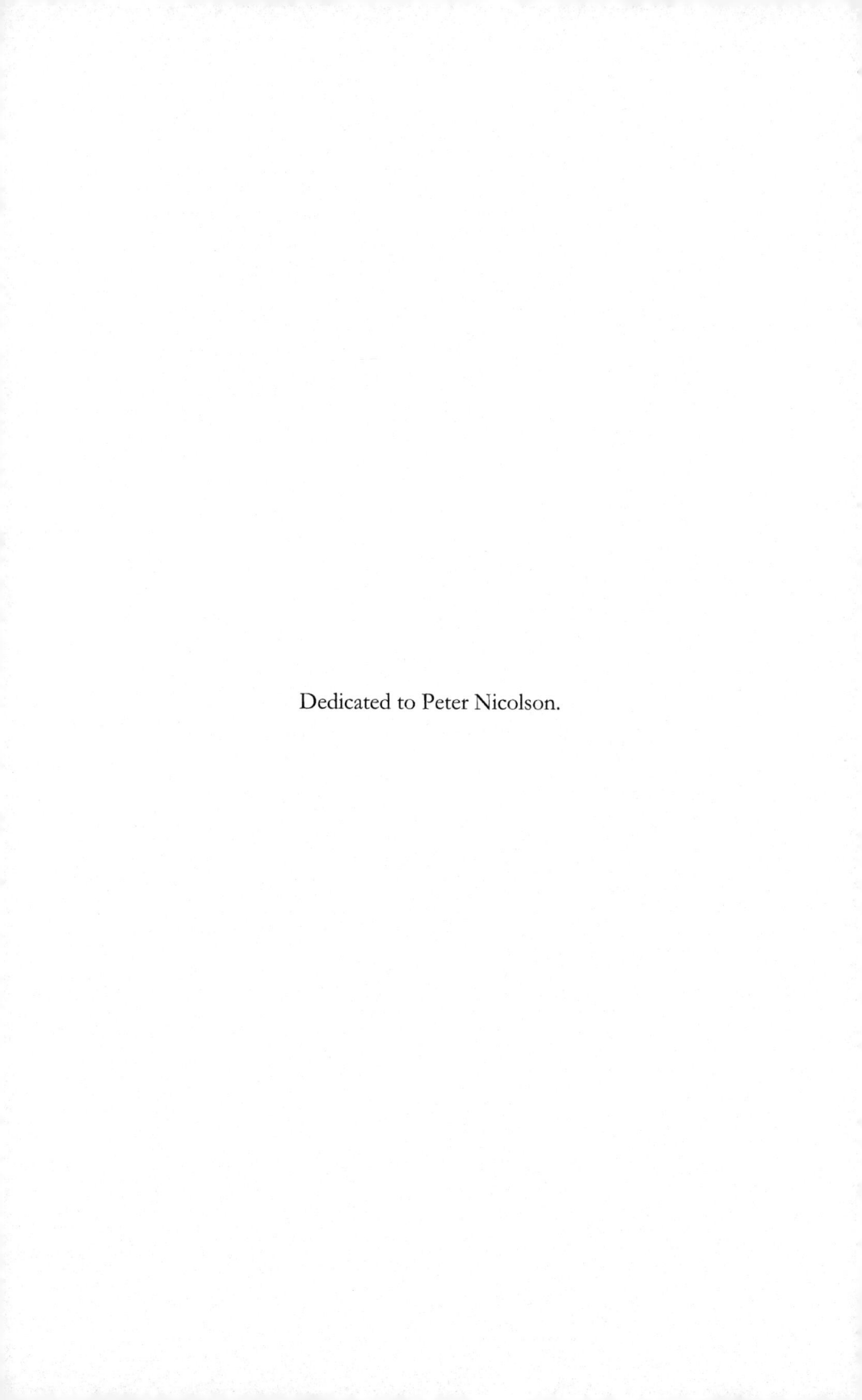

CONTENTS

	Acknowledgments	i
	Foreword	1
	Introduction	3
1	Joy Unspeakable	5
2	The Spirit and The Word	9
3	Going Public	12
4	Gifts for Today	16
5	Gospel Tools	21
6	Restoring the Ministry to the Church	27
7	Understanding the Baptism in the Holy Spirit	33
8	Tongues	38
9	Prophecy	43
10	Pentecost and the Local Church	49
11	Preparing for Pentecost	53
12	Experiencing Pentecost	58
13	Beyond Pentecost	62

ACKNOWLEDGMENTS

I am grateful to the copyright sources of the works quoted in this publication for permission granted to use their work. Except for these quotations, any part of this publication may be quoted or reproduced freely and without request or restriction.

Unless otherwise stated, biblical quotations are from the New American Standard Bible Copyright 1960, 1962, 1963, 1968, 1971, 1972, 1973, 1975, 1977 by The Lockman Foundation.

Special thanks to Jean Munn for her administrative expertise and ensuring copyright requirements were all met; to Barbara for her patience; to my late Mum, Neil Paterson, and Kay Newman for proof reading; to Samuel McKibben, John Yeoman (late), Alex Gillies and Andrew Purdie (late) for their contributions; and to Donny Stewart and Donald Buchanan for all their encouragement.

This publication is not a revision but, except for the title change from *Highland Pentecost* and back-cover descriptor, a reprint of the May 2001 original edition.

FOREWORD

I've just paused at the roadside by Loch Maree on my way to Gairloch for another day's work to reflect on the purpose of this little book. In recent years, I've travelled tens of thousands of miles around bends and over hills all over the West Highlands and Islands, weaving through the Cuillins and skirting Loch Dunvegan, gazing over the Sound of Rona towards the Torridon hills from North Skye, and then with satisfaction taking in the Trotternish peninsula from the mountain roads high on the other side. I've stared out at the stacks of St Kilda from Balivanich on a clear day and watched the sheer force of Atlantic rollers pounding tiny Dalbeg Bay on the west side of Lewis. On numerous occasions, bobbing along Hebridean single track roads, I've thought back to previous years spent in Glasgow and smiled to myself, *this sure beats the Clyde Tunnel!*

But then I think of the words of a song by Ian White lamenting "scenery of plenty, but no Spirit's blaze", and agree that without argument I would trade all this for something much more grand ... a visit from God, something that would impact every town and village of the Highlands and Islands. To the Christian, great panoramas and seascapes, though marvellous displays of God's handiwork, are peripheral to God's creation; the centre of God's concern is people and their needs. Hidden from view in these Highland glens are the manic depressive and the alcoholic, families torn in two, and a new generation with no reason to expect anything from the church. Human need is not confined to urban housing schemes. As a Christian living in a scenic paradise, I have to regularly remind myself that this is why I am here.

Also scattered around the West Highlands and Islands are some beacons of hope, shining testimonies who have so much to offer in a region that desperately needs something new from God.

There have been some rare flickers of light, like old Peter Nicolson of Staffin, who recently passed away, and others who still shine brightly today. Their example spurs me to put this into print.

Alistair J Matheson, May 2001

As can be deduced from the above foreword, my original manuscript was written and intended for the West Highland and Island context in which I then lived. I was engaged in planting a Pentecostal/charismatic church in a Christian culture that was largely conservative and Presbyterian, making me something of a strange new animal who needed to provide a measure of biblical explanation. I ran off 1,000 copies and, when the boxes finally emptied, I considered it job done.

I had not an inkling that 22 years later I would pick up an old copy, having discarded my original manuscript, and republish – not this time mainly for a Reformed, decidedly cessationist readership but, stingingly, for a wider audience of 'Pentecostals' who have forgotten Pentecost and 'charismatics' who have lost the charismata.

With this new, broadened audience in mind and in with a sense of haste – like Paul (Acts 20:16), I was keen to get this one done 'in time for Pentecost'! – the only noticeable changes I have made to the first edition have been in reference to the localised Highland context of the original.

Alistair J Matheson, May 2023

INTRODUCTION

The conviction that drove me to write *Empowered: The Baptism in the Holy Spirit* is drawn from both the abundantly clear teaching of the New Testament and the experiences of countless Christian believers.

It has from time to time been cautioned by evangelicals that Christians should seek to embrace truth rather than experience. But how can any truth that is able to detach itself from experience be relevant to life? The separation of truth and experience is unrealistic: biblical truth leads to and demands experience, and this book has been written because the New Testament requires all Christians to be "clothed" with the power of God (Luke 24:49).

The word `Pentecostal' traces its origins to the Day of Pentecost recorded in Acts chapter 2, when the first believers were baptised with the Holy Spirit and began to speak in other unlearned tongues and bear witness to Jesus Christ with great boldness by the Holy Spirit's inspiration. This Pentecostal baptism became the initiation into Christian service for converts throughout the Book of Acts. Modern-day Pentecostals have discovered through scripture and experience that the baptism with the Holy Spirit and its accompanying phenomena have never changed or become obsolete.

The word 'charismatic' is derived from the Greek New Testament word 'charismata', which is translated 'gifts.' Extraordinary spiritual gifts, such as speaking in tongues, prophecy, and healing, were commonplace in the ministry of the New Testament church. The modern Charismatic Movement, which over the latter part of the 20th century swept through virtually all

Christian denominations, brought with it the rediscovery that God never did withdraw the charismatic gifts from His church.

Although the terms 'Pentecostal' and 'charismatic' have inevitably become labels of attachment to various denominations and churches, these terms in their pure meaning relate to the same spiritual experience, the baptism with the Holy Spirit. This sermon-on-paper seeks not to promote a denomination, but an experience. There is no subtext, only the anticipation that, as the church of Jesus Christ continues to return to her inheritance, an explanation of Pentecost will be increasingly demanded.

The greatest need of our communities is for the church of Jesus Christ to experience an empowering of the Holy Spirit, an outpouring of repentance and faith, of salvation and healing, of spiritual fruit and spiritual gifts. Not selected parts, but the whole provision!

At the dawn of a third millennium, the future is full of hope for any church willing to step onto the pages of the New Testament, retrace its steps and retrieve the Pentecostal birth right. *"Remember therefore from where you have fallen, and repent and do the deeds you did at first ..."* (Revelation 2:5). It's back to the future!

1 JOY UNSPEAKABLE

"The young Prince [Britannicus, brother of Nero] ... felt as if a Power and a Presence stronger than his own dominated his being; annihilated his inmost self; dealt with him as a player does who sweeps the strings of an instrument into concord or discord at his will. He felt ashamed of the impulse; he felt terrified by it; but it breathed all over and around and through him, like the mighty wind; it filled his soul as with ethereal fire; it seemed to inspire, to uplift, to dilate his very soul; and finally it swept him onward as with numberless rushings of congregated wings."

Dean Farrar[1]

I will never forget the first time I experienced a charismatic meeting. Although I had now been a Christian for eight months, what I saw opened up to me a completely new world of Christian experience.

Despite the fact that the modern Pentecostal Movement began at the turn of the 20th century and the Charismatic Movement in the late-1950s, before 1982 I had never even heard of either. Having been raised in a fairly stiff Highland Calvinistic tradition, entering a charismatic church was something of a culture shock for me!

---

[1] Dean Farrar, *Darkness to Dawn*, renders an account of Britannicus' visit to a Christian meeting in first century Rome.

I had become aware of a lively young fellowship in the West End of Glasgow through a friend called Chris. From the first time I saw him, Chris had struck me as different from most other Christians I knew. The thing that really stood out about him was that, for a Christian, he seemed remarkably unashamed of his faith! I secretly longed for the natural-ness and liberty I saw in his life as he so openly shared his faith with others. And it was partly this longing that took me along to his church one Sunday morning.

Now some of us, particularly those of a more conservative outlook, are often fearful and sceptical of anything that is *different*. There is a part in all of us that feels secure in an environment where everything is quantifiable, predictable, and controllable. The older we get, the more difficult the unknown becomes to accommodate. But I had youth on my side, and I instantly knew that this was something I couldn't turn aside from.

It is no overstatement to say that what I witnessed in that place was to revolutionise my Christian life. Here was a church where an order of service was virtually impossible to recognise, and yet where the presence of God was to so grip me for an absorbing two-plus hours that seemed more like twenty minutes. It was unlike anything I had ever experienced.

As I looked around me that Sunday morning, I saw over a hundred faces, many of them no older than mine, lost in wonder, eyes often closed, arms stretched upwards, hearts and minds totally engaged, singing together as one. They were genuine. It was real. These faces were shining. What's more, they seemed quite oblivious to the fact that I was watching – most unlike church!

These people were totally immersed in worshipping God. They looked to be completely given to Jesus, and unashamedly so. I had never before seen such joy radiate so freely from the faces of Christians. This must be what the Bible called "joy unspeakable".

As I watched them worshipping, they seemed to be in heaven, and yet for me they were bringing heaven to earth. I must admit, even for a seeker like me the other-worldliness of it all was quite scary! But such fears were allayed and dispelled by the assurance and peace that exuded from them. I thought to myself over and over again, *This must be what it was like in the beginning.*

There was no hymn board at the front of the hall - I don't think anyone would have noticed it even if there had been! And yet they sang harmoniously from one song to the next, as if being led by an invisible conductor. Sunday by Sunday, coherent themes would emerge through their often-spontaneous worship. Every meeting was a new learning experience, an adventure; this actually made my Hebridean psyche feel quite guilty initially – a part of me felt as if such enjoyment did not even belong to Sunday, let alone church!

I would sit amazed as the pastor invariably spoke on the same matters introduced through the praise, and yet he had come to the meeting with no more knowledge than anyone else of what songs were going to be sung, or of how others would contribute. Had I been of a more sceptical disposition, I might well have asked, 'Has this been rigged?' Although I was unable to articulate such a wonderful principle back then, I soon came to realise that God intends the coming together of His people in itself to produce a dynamic out of which He delights to speak.

Such a principle conflicts with today's Western, individualistic model of church ministry, whereby the church gathers together to be spoken to, not through. The focus of church life has centred upon the individual rather than the community, and the greatest monument of our individualism has been the one-man-ministry. What a far cry from the early church, where they met together day by day, *"breaking bread from house to house"*[2] and encouraging one another *"with psalms and hymns and spiritual songs"*[3], where *"each one has a psalm, has a teaching, has a revelation, has a tongue, has an interpretation"*[4], where the river of God's blessings and gifts was poured out, causing table-servers to preach and preachers to wash feet.

During my first weeks at this new church, it became very apparent that the preacher wasn't the only one who came prepared to minister. At the height of worship, different ones would stand up and read from the Scriptures or pray heartily. Someone else might walk to the front, whisper something in the pastor's ear and then start to relate a prophetic word or vision that he or she had received while worshipping. Others, obviously more experienced in these gifts, might stand where they were and deliver clear, specific words of encouragement which perhaps only applied to two or three individuals in the

---

[2] Acts 2:46.
[3] Ephesians 5:19.
[4] I Corinthians 14:26.

meeting. There might even be 'words of knowledge', where it was revealed that somebody present had some kind of need which would be met through the laying on of hands, or simply through the receiving of the word.

As these gifts were in operation, I would discreetly look around me and occasionally see faces break into a grin which seemed to say either that God had shown them the same thing, or that they personally needed to hear what had just been said. Others would bow their heads quietly as they realised that God was dealing with them, gently but firmly. It was not an uncommon thing for people to stand up and add personal confirmation to a word that had just been given.

Another thing that intrigued me was tongues. Someone would speak out in a language that could sound like anything from Mandarin to Italian to Apache (– not that I speak any of them!). And then, what really amazed me was that someone else would stand up and give an interpretation to what had just been said. Then another would nod in agreement that this was the interpretation they had too! I was quite transfixed by the whole thing. Clock-watching was certainly not a problem – I would sit there for over two hours, and at the close I would not want to go home. Indeed, sometimes the meeting just didn't seem able to end as the 'closing song' would lead into another half hour or more of high praises. During those weeks I was to experience all the emotions of a Peter being beckoned to step out of the boat!

The meetings flowed in harmony and unity, always with congregational participation. You left with no doubt as to what God was saying to you personally, and, more importantly, with an increased hunger to search the scriptures when you got home. God had touched your life and may well have touched other lives through you – if He hadn't, there was a good likelihood of Him doing so over the next few days!

I had discovered Pentecost.

2 THE SPIRIT AND THE WORD

"My message and my preaching were not in persuasive words of wisdom, but in demonstration of the Spirit and of power, that your faith should not rest in the wisdom of men, but on the power of God."

The Apostle Paul[5]

Through the Pentecostal movements of the twentieth century, there was a remarkable restoration of the gifts of the Spirit. Many witnessed the transformational effect of the word of God being united with displays of the Spirit's power. Just as the truth gains impact through demonstration, so also genuine demonstration finds its purpose in the truth.

As with anything that is good in life, however, there is a danger with the gifts of the Spirit that we begin to latch onto the gifts themselves above the One who gives them. As soon as we do this, we start to lose our spiritual perspective and purpose. Although God desires us to know His acts of power, it is our personal relationship with Him that is of greatest importance. *"Do not rejoice in this, that the spirits are subject to you,"* Jesus told His disciples, *"But rejoice that your names are recorded in heaven."*[6]

Some charismatics have been accused of jettisoning the scriptures in the

---

[5] I Corinthians 2:4-5.
[6] Luke 10:20.

pursuit of other revelations and experiences. If they have done this, then it is certainly not the fault of the Holy Spirit. Jesus said that the Spirit would lead us into all the truth. An outstanding mark of anyone who is truly filled with the Holy Spirit is a deep hunger for the word of God.

I am thankful for the biblical heritage I received through the evangelical upbringing of my childhood. It laid in me a deep and unquestioning respect for the Scriptures, a respect that I have come to recognise as foundational to my Christian life.

Foundations are so important. Above the ground's surface, two houses might look identical, but if one has no foundation beneath it, then it is not going to pass the test of time. The houses may have been built by the same hands, using the same materials, but if one of them has nothing below to support it, then weights, pressures and movements will eventually cause it to crumble.

I do not remember ever not knowing about sin and salvation – throughout my earliest years, I think I had a fairly good idea of where I stood in relation to both! In common with many other families from a similar background, every day we had family worship, when the Scriptures were read, and we were led in prayer.

I can still vividly remember one school holiday on the Isle of Tiree, taking the best part of a cruelly sunny Sunday afternoon to memorise the marathon answer to the eighteenth question of the Shorter Catechism of the Westminster Confession of Faith: "Wherein consisteth the sinfulness of that estate whereinto man fell?" How I wished Adam had never sinned! Such exercises were far from pleasurable at the time, but their value was for the future.

When I became a Christian as an eighteen-year-old student, nobody had to explain to me the way of salvation or teach me a 'sinner's prayer'. I had come to a place of brokenness which was based upon the clear understanding that I was a sinner justifiably condemned by God's law, and I knew that my repentance and faith would see a sovereign work of God's grace take place in my life.

What had been dead words immediately became a source of life. My early grounding in the Scriptures, at the moment of my conversion, suddenly became a vital foundation, instantly imbuing me with unshakeable biblical principles which, in turn, would provide me with priceless spiritual resources from the very first stages of my Christian walk and throughout my life. Thank God for the foundations of His word!

I have never heard a Pentecostal preacher remotely suggest that miraculous phenomena should ever take the place of the word of God. The erosion of absolute trust in the full inspiration of the Scriptures is a modern trend, which finds its origins not in the charismatic and Pentecostal movements, but in the liberal wings of established churches. I do not say this to defend the Pentecostal movements or to condemn others, but to illustrate the fact that Pentecostal phenomena do not compete with or take away from a dependency on scripture; rather they compel people back to the book which gives them their reason.

"We preach Christ crucified," Paul declared to the Corinthians, *"to Jews a stumbling block, and to Gentiles foolishness."*[7] And he went on to reveal the secret of the gospel's early success, *"... My message and my preaching were not in persuasive words of wisdom, but in demonstration of the Spirit and of power, that your faith should not rest on the wisdom of men, but on the power of God."*[8]

Thank God for the foundation of scripture which so unglamorously undergirds our Christian heritage. Add the power of Pentecost and you have very potent mix indeed. If the power of the Holy Spirit ever detonates the Bible knowledge that is still stockpiled in some of our churches and communities, there could be an explosion greater magnitude than any of us might dare to predict!

The trouble with explosions, however, is that they cannot be tidily contained, much less kept private!

---

[7] I Corinthians 1:23.
[8] I Corinthians 2:4-5.

3 GOING PUBLIC

"I am destined to proclaim the message, unmindful of personal consequences to myself."

Nikolaus Ludwig Von Zinzendorf

As the Protestant Reformation struggled unsuccessfully to change the spiritual landscape of sixteenth century France, John Calvin frustratedly denounced the phenomenon of Nicodemitism. Nicodemitism was the practice of a number of closet evangelicals who, like Nicodemus, outwardly conformed to the religious practices of the day, but continued to meet clandestinely by night in the secrecy of their homes.

As far as Calvin was concerned, these frightened Christians were betraying the cause. Many of those who welcomed the Reformation message to their parlours, never quite managed to transport it to pulpit or pew. Had they all made a public, united stand from the outset, who knows that the terrible blood baths of the French Inquisition might not have been averted?

Many similar historical illustrations serve a very important point: there must always be a distinction between personal and private. A Christian's faith is a deeply personal thing, but it must never be allowed to become a private thing. The gospel must never be confined by the fear of man. God blesses people in order to make them a blessing – and just as it cost Christ, it will cost us too!

I have a friend in the city of Minsk, Belarus, called Benjamin Bruch. Benjamin originally came from Kiev in the Ukraine, where he was a committed member of an unregistered church under the Communist regime. Things went well for him in the church until he received the baptism with the Holy Spirit and started speaking in tongues. The response of the church was that, unless he forsook these strange practices, he would no longer be allowed to preach. But Benjamin knew that he could not deny what God had given him, and he told the elders that, if they would not let him preach in the church, then he would have to go out into the open air and preach there.

Benjamin was only too well aware of what this might mean. His great-grandfather had been executed for his faith, his grandfather had been taken away to be shot only to be unexpectedly released, and his wife's uncle had been martyred under Brezhnev. So, with his heart pounding, he went out into the city square the following Sunday, accompanied by two friends. As he started to preach, a crowd gathered. But then, inevitably, the militia arrived. Realising that this could be his last opportunity to publicly preach the gospel, Benjamin carried on with even greater fervour!

After he finished, the two armed officers walked up to him and, appearing quite moved, told him that, since he was the only one doing anything to prevent crime in the city, he was free to preach the gospel there every Sunday, for as long as he wished! The last time I heard, in September of 1995, that work was still continuing, led by Benjamin's father, with a congregation of two hundred meeting every Sunday of the year in a public park (with no winter break from the sub-zero temperatures!).

What was it that drove Benjamin, at the risk of losing his freedom, his family, and perhaps even his life, out into the most public of places to preach the Gospel?

Jesus said, *"You shall receive power when the Holy Spirit has come upon you; and you shall be My witnesses...."*[9] Our word 'martyrs' comes from the Greek 'martures', which is here translated 'witnesses'. The Pentecostal baptism was and is the empowerment which enables the church to boldly profess Jesus Christ,

---

[9] Acts 1:8.

whatever the cost. It is one of the greatest needs of the church today.

Consider what it did for the first church. From the Day of Pentecost onwards, the same believers who, only weeks before, had failed to stand with their master when he needed them most, became an ever-growing, fearless band who went everywhere they could, *"turning the world upside-down"*[10]. They had so recently been left brow-beaten, demoralised, and confident only of their own impotence. But here they were, suddenly catapulted out into the city streets, country roads, and right across the Mediterranean world. What made the difference?

What was the difference between the Peter who swore he never knew Jesus, and the brazen radical who fearlessly challenged the rulers of the Jews to decide for themselves whether he ought to obey them or God?

The Book of Acts makes it abundantly clear that it was the baptism in the Holy Spirit that so dramatically transformed the first disciples.

So, what about today's church? Whom does it most closely resemble – the pre-Pentecost disciples or the post-Pentecostals? Are our evangelical churches more like Samson – a great history, but shorn, weak and humiliated today?

Some people teach that every Christian has received the baptism with the Holy Spirit at conversion. If that is the case, then we would have to conclude that a sizeable percentage of evangelical Christians in our churches have never, in fact, been converted. The result of the baptism in the Holy Spirit has always been an unmistakable boldness and liberty in bearing witness to Jesus Christ.

Everywhere they went, the first church fearlessly proclaimed Jesus, despite being insulted, mocked, slandered, beaten, imprisoned, banished, and martyred. The believers in Acts counted the cost, received the power, nailed their reputations and earthly securities to the cross, and gave themselves to the gospel. We know very little of the price they had to pay, and yet God is still having to call many of us out of the closet today.

I've heard some Christians say, with an impressive degree of martyrdom in

---

[10] Acts 17:6.

their voices, *"I'm afraid it might take a wave of persecution to revive the church in this land."* I couldn't disagree more. No intelligent anti-Christian force would dream of persecuting a sleeping church! Why would the devil spoil a good thing?! We've got it the wrong way around. It will take a revival to bring about persecution – persecution is this world's reward for Pentecost! That's precisely why many in the church don't want Pentecost. Once the church is mobilised by the power of the Holy Spirit and finds itself treading on touchy toes, then it's time to expect a rough ride!

The trouble is we're mostly in a comfort zone. We're too respectable. We've horded social capital and have accumulated too much to lose (we think!). But, as I once heard somebody quip, if God is going to comfort the afflicted of this world, then first He must afflict the comfortable in the church! If the world around us is ever going to be turned upside-down for Jesus, then the church needs to be turned inside-out – and that is what brings us to the baptism in the Holy Spirit.

Why be ruled by what people might think, or by what might happen to our image? Why not just hand it all over to God? Why not allow Him to bring us out from behind our hiding places of convention and acceptability? (How much are we really respected for being there anyway?) Why not go public in the power of Pentecost?

The power of Pentecost, however, is about more than courage, boldness, and a martyr spirit.

4 GIFTS FOR TODAY

"Take up the instruments that Paul laid down when he laid down his life for Jesus' sake. Take up the instruments that made the early church mighty in God. Take up the instruments that Jesus used – that He promised to all who should believe for them."

Harold Horton[11]

Feeling the wounds on a woman's head one day made me feel like the disciple Thomas. It wasn't that I didn't believe but experiencing this lady's testimony put me in touch once again with the God of the impossible. Elizabeth, a sprightly seventy-something, had invited me to run my finger right along the protruding scars just above her forehead hairline and behind both her ears. I felt the pronounced ridges where the tumours had split her skull open. Blind, carrying a morphine drip, and in the final stages of 'incurable' cancer, Elizabeth's life was saved by her faith in Jesus' power to heal. For many years since that miracle, she has travelled the world, preaching the Good News and healing the sick, just as Jesus instructed His disciples in the beginning.

Religious people of Jesus' day didn't seem to have any great problem with His healing of the sick; their difficulty was with His claim to forgive sins. Modern cessationism seems to have turned the tables: whilst Christ's power

---

[11] Harold Horton, The Gifts of the Spirit, tenth edition (Assemblies of God Publishing House, 1976), *p.* 204.

to forgive sins is embraced with reverence, His ministry of the miraculous has been largely consigned to legend. I can understand non-believers rejecting the supernatural – at least they're consistent – but I cannot fathom it in those who claim to be Bible-believing Christians. Why would He be able to – and desire to – heal then, and not today?

Jesus commissioned His followers, saying, *"Go into all the world and preach the gospel to all creation. He who has believed and has been baptised shall be saved; but he who has disbelieved shall be condemned. And these signs will accompany those who have believed: in My name they will cast out demons, they will speak with new tongues; they will pick up serpents, and if they drink any deadly poison, it shall not hurt them; they will lay hands on the sick, and they will recover."*[12]

Why should the first two of these three sentences apply today, but the third not? If, as some have ventured to argue, these gifts were only required for the initial launch of the church, why is there no foundation for such a theory in the writings of the New Testament itself?

Some have labelled this vaguely and variously defined launching period the 'apostolic age'. The reasoning seems to be that at the close of such a period (perhaps the end of the ministry span of the Twelve, with the add-on of that enigma Paul who even then played havoc with cessationism's clean-cut definitions of what an apostle was!) the gifts were called back to heaven. (If only we knew the date of old John's death, then we could commemorate a kind of Retro-Pentecost Day!)

So, what does this word 'apostolic' mean? The Greek 'apostolos' simply meant 'sent one'. If it has a pure meaning, the phrase 'apostolic age' must be the 'sending age'. This begs the question, when did God stop sending? The gifts were really not given to personalities, but to a task; the original personalities are long gone, but the task is most certainly not complete. As far as the clarity of Christ's purposes is concerned, if there is such a thing as an 'apostolic age', then it can only be defined as the church age. And the church, that glorious collective of all God's Spirit-born children (– He has no grandchildren), according to the apostle Peter (I, 2:9), is only one generation.

If the charismatic gifts were at some point withdrawn, surely such a

---

[12] Mark 16:15-18.

significant event would have been predicted by the New Testament writers, recognised, and recorded by the early fathers, and at least merited a brief mention in the annals of ancient church history. How else, for example, would the tongue-speaking Waldensians of the thirteenth century know they weren't being misled? Today's sceptics have used the relative silence of the works of early church history, read through spectacles of unbelief, to justify a cessationist theology that has no substance in the New Testament.

Surely those who assert that these supernatural effects are not for today ought to be able to tell us for just how long this has been the case? Actually, the New Testament does clearly tell us when the gifts are to be done away: *"when the perfect comes"*[13]. In a future age of glory, they will no longer be required. As we have seen, Jesus did not designate the gifts solely for the equipping of apostles, first century disciples, or any other privileged historical or ethnic group, but broadly for *"those who have believed"*[11]. So, the real question is, how many believers does Jesus have today – Christians who will embrace the whole counsel of scripture, no picking and choosing, with simple and consistent faith?

Some might argue that, if it is true that these sign gifts are still available to the church today, then why are they not being seen in our churches? Firstly, it must be said that they are occurring (although far more frequently in non-Western regions), albeit in an incredibly unpublicised way. Secondly, if we hold a high view of scripture, we will not allow our faith in its promises to be limited by what we may or may not personally have experienced – God's power at work requires our faith in action. And thirdly, the reason for the scarcity of the gifts has been precisely the same as the reason for the lack of liberty and boldness in our witness, which we considered in the last chapter – we have become strangers to the fullness with the Holy Spirit. The truth is that it was not only the gifts of the Spirit that were to disappear with the institutionalisation of the church, but boldness and zeal as well – did God 'withdraw' these also?

On the subject of spiritual gifts, the eighteenth-century revivalist, John Wesley, had this to say: *"The cause of [the disappearance of the gifts] was not (as has been vulgarly supposed) 'because there was no occasion for them' because all the world was become Christian. This is a miserable mistake: not a twentieth part of it was then nominally*

---

[13] I Corinthians 13:10.

Christian. The real cause was: 'the love of many' – almost of all Christians, so called – was 'waxed cold'. The Christians had no more of the Spirit of Christ than the other heathens. This was the real cause why the extraordinary gifts of the Holy Ghost were no longer found in the Christian church – because the Christians were turned heathen again, and had only a dead form left."[14]

Well!

Wesley brings us to the heart of the matter: the matter of the heart. The absence of the gifts of the Spirit from the church is not a mark of God's 'good pleasure', but rather a barometer of our hardness of heart and unbelief. We have become like the Nazareth of Jesus' day, where *"He could do no miracle ... except that He laid His hands upon a few sick people and healed them. And He wondered at their unbelief."*[15]

Why would God strip the church of such powerful resources when there was still so much to be accomplished? Would a general send his army into battle, and then relieve it of a vital part of its armoury when the fight was only beginning to get underway? There are more people living without any knowledge of Christ in our generation than at any other time in history. If the power of Pentecost was needed in the first century, then how much more as we journey into the third millennium!

Remember Moses in Pharaoh's court when the magicians of Egypt turned their rods into serpents? Did Moses look on and think, I wish I could do that! Not quite! God gave Moses a power that confounded their powers, a staff that swallowed up their staffs. In our day, with the proliferation of the occult and all kinds of supernatural phenomena on an enormous scale, it is almost as if the other isms are taunting the church, saying, "Where's your power, then?" Has Christ left His church without an answer? In a generation when millions of people are being sucked into alternative spiritual experiences, the church had better have more to offer the world than theology and ritual.

'Ah,' comes the response, 'But the greatest miracle we can ever see is a soul coming to Christ.' I for one wholeheartedly agree and, if there had to be a choice, I would rather see one soul experiencing that joy than the entire world

---

[14] "The More Excellent Way" [The Works of John Wesley, ed. Albert C. Outler (Nashville: Abingdon Press, 1986), 3:263-264].
[15] Mark 6:5-6.

miraculously restored to physical health for a breath of time on earth, but the fact is that Jesus never separated the two. As it was in Christ's earthly ministry, God means us to have both – it was never intended to be a case of one or the other. When Jesus sent the disciples out, He commanded them to preach the gospel *and* heal the sick. The healing ministry accompanied, illustrated, and amplified the message preached. It resulted in more souls being reached. It still does today.

Recent decades have seen the most expansive spiritual awakening in the history of Christianity in Asia, Latin America, and Africa, through Spirit-filled believers who have discovered that Christ is continuing every aspect of His earthly ministry through His church today.

But if we want to understand how Christ desires to work in our time, we don't have to travel all the way to Korea or Argentina; all we have to do is turn again to the Gospels and the Book of Acts.

5 GOSPEL TOOLS

"And a great multitude was following Him, because they were seeing the signs which He was performing on those who were sick."

The Gospel of John[16]

In his book *Power Evangelism*[17], John Wimber related an experience he had on a flight between Chicago and New York. As he reclined on his seat, hoping for a relaxing journey, he looked across the aisle and suddenly saw the word 'ADULTERY' written over a middle-aged man! He blinked, rubbed his eyes, and sat shocked as it dawned on him that God was showing him something.

When the man saw that Wimber was staring at him, he turned round and snapped, "What do you want?"

Just then, the name 'Jane' came into Wimber's mind. "Does the name 'Jane' mean anything to you?"

The man turned ashen and stammered, "We've got to talk."

The two men went to the cocktail lounge, where – to cut a long story short – the man broke down in front of staff and passengers in tears of repentance

---

[16] John 6:2.
[17] *Power Evangelism: Signs and Wonders Today*; John Wimber with Kevin Springer; Hodder & Stoughton, 1985.

and committed his life to Christ.

The man then returned to his seat and explained to his stunned wife what had just happened, confessing his affair, and asking for her forgiveness. She too accepted Christ, and they left the aeroplane with Wimber's Bible.

The dynamics of Wimber's encounter are basically the same as the meeting between Jesus and the woman at the well in Samaria, related in John chapter 4. The woman was showing little sign of appreciating spiritual truth until Jesus suddenly commanded her attention by means of a revealing glimpse into her personal life. Then, immediately, she starts to "perceive" that He is a prophet. And before John leaves the story, he tells us that many Samaritans believed because of the woman's testimony.

But what was it that the woman told the people of Sychar that brought them to Christ? Had she discovered a wonderful, eloquent communicator? Had she found a great teacher with the soundest doctrine ever to visit Samaria? I do not doubt that these would have been true, but these are not the things that brought that city to Christ. The woman simply testified, "He told me all the things that I have done."[18] Time and again in Jesus' ministry, it is extraordinary spiritual gifts that bring down all kinds of barriers of resistance and open up lives to the message He preaches.

If we removed the miraculous from the ministry of Jesus and the first believers, then the prose of the Gospels and Acts would start to seem comparatively bare. Before the church began to stray from her first love, it never occurred to her to divorce the miracles from the message. Preaching the gospel of the kingdom and healing the sick went hand in hand, as inseparable as paint and brush, nail and hammer.

When Jesus preached, He did not depend upon the historical authenticity of the miracles of Moses and Elijah to confirm His message. And when the apostles went out, they didn't have to rely on the signs their master had performed the previous week to confirm their preaching .... *"They went out and preached everywhere, while the Lord worked with them, and confirmed the word by the signs that followed."*[19] They simply preached the word, with signs following.

---

[18] John 4:39.
[19] Mark 16:20.

Today, we read the miracles of Jesus, with preaching following! But miracles are not essentially for preaching about – they are for performing. God's pattern for evangelising every generation is for His word to be preached with its own signs following. Even in supposed 'Christian' countries, we are surrounded by countless unevangelised 'Samaritans' whose attentions demand to be claimed.

The most immediate challenge facing most Western churches today is not to communicate a message, but rather to find an audience! As on the Day of Pentecost, something has to happen in and through the church that will cause the world around us to look and start asking, *"What does this mean?"*[20] Then we will have people to preach to.

Why does it have to be this way? Because when we open the Bible to preach, the world needs to know that the God we are talking about is not merely a God of history, now confined to the pages of a work of antiquity. If Jesus does not heal the sick today, why should unbelievers who are far from convinced of the 'full, plenary inspiration' of the Scriptures trust us when we tell them that He did it two thousand years ago? We are, after all, telling them that He is still alive. If Jesus *does* today what He did then, it will surely be easier for them to believe that He *says* today what He said then.

The first church knew exactly what it meant to continue the earthly ministry of Jesus. One day in the temple, all the people saw a man whom they had previously known as a beggar and a cripple causing quite a stir, leaping about and praising God. What had happened in his life to cause him to praise God with such exuberance? He had simply met two Christians who knew what Christ was able to do for him. They had boldly commanded him: *"Look at us!"*[21]

Now, that is not what we say. We say, *'Don't look at us – look to the Lord!'* It sounds spiritual, but it also enables us to evade responsibility. Such an attitude cannot be fully pleasing to Jesus because He has sent us to be His representatives. Jesus Christ has delegated His earthly ministry and imparted His anointing to His church in order that the world might see Him *by* looking at us. The rulers of the Jews were later able to *"recognise [Peter and John] as having*

---

[20] Acts 2:12.
[21] Acts 3:4.

been with Jesus."[22] To Peter and John, the whole purpose of looking at them was to see Jesus! When the world looks at us today, do they just see us, or do they also see Jesus, the Saviour, Healer, and Deliverer?

Then, we read that the man looked at them expectantly, but he surely did not anticipate what he was about to hear. Peter said, *"I do not possess silver and gold, but **what I do have** I give to you: In the name of Jesus Christ the Nazarene – walk!"*[23] (Emphasis mine)

The man probably had many spiritual needs, but Peter and John knew the key to his life. They saw the man's most obvious physical need, and they knew that they had the tool for the job. They knew that healing was not merely a supplement to the gospel ministry – it was a part of it. And when the man was healed, it was more than his body that was touched.

I will never forget the time in a Glasgow church where I once served when a visiting preacher announced, by the inspiration of the Holy Spirit, that there was someone in the congregation who had been paralysed on one side of his body in a car accident. The preacher declared in faith that, if the person came forward, he would be healed.

The congregation sat in suspense as a man, a taxi driver, from near the back of the hall, began to make his way to the front. After receiving prayer, he began to rotate his previously immobile upper left arm. But what will always live in my memory is the sight of him taking off running around the hall and being met halfway by his friend who had come to the meeting with him. These two Glasgow men, without airs and graces, embraced one another with tears running down their faces. As I stood there amidst a deeply moved congregation, all of whom were by this point on their feet applauding, I thought of the lame man in the temple.

As we look around our communities, there are so many lives that could be opened to Jesus by such a touch. Like the demoniac whom Jesus healed and sent away *"to proclaim in Decapolis what great things Jesus had done for him"*[24], whole communities could be sparked into spiritual awareness by just one miracle. An audience would start to gather, and many who thought the church was

---

[22] Acts 4:13.
[23] Acts 3:6.
[24] Mark 5:20.

little more than a charitable institution with nice people (hopefully!) would stop and start asking and listening.

Before He healed a paralytic one day, Jesus told some sceptical scribes, *"In order that you may know that the Son of Man has authority on earth to forgive sins, ... I say to you, rise, take up your pallet and go home."*[25] Have unbelievers become so much more spiritual than in the days of Jesus that they no longer need demonstrations to prove that Christ does indeed have the power to forgive sins?

Some say that we no longer need miracles because we've got the New Testament. But just think what that kind of logic is saying: The Living Word Himself required signs to accompany His preaching; but us, no, we don't need them – we've got His words in a book! The word and the signs were never intended to substitute one another, but to complement one another. Miracles are no more in competition with the written Word today than they were in the ministry of Jesus.

We have a gentleman in our church, called Andrew, who never ceases to give testimony to how he came to meet Jesus as his Saviour. After two months of incessant muscular pains and swelling that his medication was unable to alleviate, he entered a Pentecostal meeting one evening. After the meeting, he was prayed for by the pastor, and what he describes as *"250 volts of electricity"* went coursing through his body. His pain left immediately, and two thorough checks by a hospital specialist over the following weeks bafflingly revealed absolutely no abnormalities.

At the same time, in the same hospital, Andrew had a friend who had been on a life support machine for five weeks. The same pastor who had prayed for Andrew told him not to worry about his friend as he would be on his feet again by the weekend. By the Saturday, he had been taken for his first walk down the ward by the nurses, who now referred to him as 'Miracle Man'.

These are more than remarkable stories; they are events that played a highly significant part in turning people into followers of Jesus.

But the gifts of the Spirit do not end with someone coming to Christ. When

---

[25] Mark 2:10-11.

people enter a local church, they are entering what the Bible calls *"the dwelling of God in the Spirit"*[26], an environment where the supernatural should not be unnatural. When the lame beggar was healed, he leaped for joy and the onlookers ran about in amazement, but it didn't appear to cause Peter and John any great excitement; for them, the expected had happened, because they had been naturalised to the world of the impossible.

In the early church and in a great many places around the world today, what Wesley referred to as the "extraordinary gifts" are commonplace. These churches demonstrate that the New Testament church is a dynamic, vibrant place to be, a place where ordinary Christians are actively engaged in extraordinary ministry by the inspiration and empowerment of the Holy Spirit.

---

[26] Ephesians 2:22.

6 RESTORING THE MINISTRY TO THE CHURCH

> *"Words like 'priest', 'minister', 'pastor' have been consistently used to describe a distinctive profession, when the New Testament uses these or similar words to describe the ministry of all the people of God. This has been pointed out many times, but the practice continues."*
>
> Michael Harper[27]

"But to each one is given the manifestation of the Spirit for the common good. For to one is given the word of wisdom through the Spirit, and to another the word of knowledge through the same Spirit; and to another faith by the same Spirit, and to another gifts of healing by the one Spirit, and to another the effecting of miracles, and to another prophecy, and to another the distinguishing of spirits, to another various kinds of tongues, and to another the interpretation of tongues. But one and the same Spirit works all these things, distributing to each one individually just as He wills."[28]

The last four words of this quotation, *"just as He wills"*, say something very important about the gifts of the Spirit. The Holy Spirit does not submit Himself to our plans! He does things like healing people in church while a sermon is still underway, or giving words of prophecy through those who are unaccustomed to speaking in public. He is the Master of unpredictability.

---

[27] Michael Harper, *Let My People Grow*, Chapter 2; Hodder & Stoughton.
[28] I Corinthians 12:7-11.

This, to some, can be quite disconcerting!

There is, however, a principle which is quite clear: if our churches are going to know the blessing of the Holy Spirit, then He must have full freedom to conduct our ministry. It is because this is quite threatening to some that the ministry of the Holy Spirit has often been strongly resisted, and the Holy Spirit has historically had to renew His activities in such unlikely and uncelebrated places as barns, upper rooms, and prison cells.

As the large part of evangelical Christianity cherished the heritage of the Protestant Reformation, assuming that all that was theologically sound would forever remain safely contained within its firmly fixed boundaries, the Holy Spirit commenced the modern-day Pentecostal revival through a one-eyed black preacher in what was described as a 'tumble-down shack' in Los Angeles in 1906.

But as the 20th century rolled on and Pentecostalism, firmly securing its capital 'P', in some places became as set in its ways as many of the denominations from which it had been ejected, in others nursing its claim to a copyright on the gifts of the Holy Spirit. Then, in 1959, the priest of a large Episcopal church began speaking in tongues. Dennis Bennett was among the first in the vanguard of what would soon be referred to as the Charismatic Movement.

Through the Charismatic Movement the gifts of the Spirit became accepted in a number of traditional churches, whilst many others either jumped or were pushed out of denominations to become independent or loosely networked fellowships. And just as many of these new churches began spreading their wings to savour their hour of destiny in the latter part of the 20th century, the Holy Spirit continued to renew His activities quite dramatically within a number of the old denominational churches again. The Holy Spirit has repeatedly demonstrated that He will not suffer exclusive claims to His power.

It is so important, as we seek the gifts of the Spirit, that we constantly keep in our minds that they are God's gifts. His is the power and His is the glory. When we lay claim to the power, it corrupts us. When we touch the glory, it burns us. When it becomes *my* or *our* ministry, we've already lost it.

The Holy Spirit is the Empowerer of the church; He is the source of all her spiritual gifts, and He is therefore the only one who can enable God's people to mature together in the use of these gifts. One of the great fundamental truths which was rediscovered through the Protestant Reformation was the priesthood of all believers – Christ had sealed this by sending His Holy Spirit to indwell every believer, not just the church's leadership. The church collectively was Christ's body. It follows, therefore, that the entire church must be mobilised in order for Christ to be adequately expressed on earth.

One of the main reasons why the Reformation had to take place was to wrest control of the church out of the grip of a corruptible ecclesiastical hierarchy. Once the Bible was translated out of Latin into the languages of the people, and its great truths began to be restored to the common believer, the Holy Spirit was enabled to take up the reins of the church again in a powerful new way.

"If God spare my life," went the famous words of William Tyndale to an English cleric of the early sixteenth century, *"ere many years pass I will cause a boy that driveth the plough shall know more of the Scriptures than thou dost."*

It would appear that what God did in the sixteenth century in relation to the Scriptures, He did in the twentieth century in relation to the gifts and ministries of the Holy Spirit. Since the middle of the second millennium, through the retrieval of the Bible to the common man, the Holy Spirit has been leading the church of Jesus Christ on a journey back to Pentecost, where every believer was actively engaged in the ministry of the church by the power of the Holy Spirit.

Had Tyndale been alive in the early twentieth century, I could imagine him visiting theological seminaries and declaring, 'Before the century's out, the layman will know more of the anointing of the Holy Spirit than you!' And how right he would have been! The recent outpourings of the Holy Spirit in the developing world surpass in power and magnitude anything that has happened on earth since the days of the first church. Not only that, but today's outpourings are coming complete with the same charismatic dimensions – tongues, prophecy, healing, and miracles. And, most significantly, the human agency has not been limited to a few, uniquely endowed ministers, but rather the mobilised masses of the body of Christ. The church has indeed been returning to Pentecost.

A phrase popularised through the Charismatic Movement was 'body ministry'. This is simply the principle that the ministry *of* the body of Christ should be carried out *by* the body of Christ, with each member exercising his or her unique gifts and callings. This is quite a contrast to the 'old model' (thankfully not the original model!), where 'the ministry' was normally kept in the domain of a professional clergy. Where body ministry is encouraged, the role of church leaders is one of enabling and equipping others for the spiritual ministry of the church, rather than doing it all themselves.

This style of leadership is thoroughly biblical. Consider, for example, the scene on the run-up to Pentecost. The preparation for the most significant event in the history of the church did not take place in a committee meeting. We find the apostles in the upper room, submerged in a gathering of 120 people, and engaged in communal prayer. And when the great baptism came, it fell indiscriminately on all – everyone together in one place. They were all filled with the Holy Spirit, and they all began to speak with other tongues.

But Peter who, as we know, was not slow at coming forward, did not stand up and shout, "Order! Order! Jesus said I was to be in charge!" – No! He was engulfed in the same outpouring as they were. Peter was simply one of the believers and the Holy Spirit was in control.

The power of the Holy Spirit was poured out upon a church where the leaders had laid down their 'golden crowns' of divine commission and come before God on the same basis as everyone else: their personal human need. These were the ones who had so recently been vying for the highest ranks in Christ's kingdom. But their imaginary little empires had perished, and now God's kingdom was coming in power. Humiliating experience had taught them that "Thy kingdom come!" means, "My kingdom go!"

However, when the right time came, and the people required a spokesman, Peter's unique gifting was brought to the fore by the inspiration of the Holy Spirit. His first sermon yielded a harvest of three thousand souls. After that, who would want their little empire back?! Today's leaders who feel threatened by the release of the church into ministry of the Holy Spirit should realise that their ministry will be enlarged rather than diminished by the gifts of others.

Wherever it arrived, the Charismatic Movement declared, *'The days of the one-*

man band are over.' That ought to come as a great relief to any sensible minister!

It may sound harsh, and I say it as someone who has at times verged on it myself, but I find it difficult to sympathise with burn-out in the ministry. Burned-out ministers not only damage themselves and make their family suffer but grieve the Holy Spirit by holding back the real growth of the church through the release and development of spiritual gifts and ministries. Perhaps the greatest epitaph to burn-out in the ministry would be, *'I did it my way!'* Jesus, by contrast, said, *"**My** yoke is easy, and **My** burden is light."*[29] (Emphasis mine.)

In his epistle to the Ephesians, Paul clearly defines the role of the leadership ministries: to so serve the church that *"the whole body, being fitted and held together by that which every joint supplies, according to the proper working of each individual part, causes the growth of the body for the building up of itself in love."*[30]

The New Testament pastor, by example, guidance and release of real responsibility, motivates the members to carry the cares and bear the burdens of the church. But it's not enough just to apply the principles of delegation – that's just creating another structure, which still requires to be filled. The 'stuff' has to be there to work with. Delegation of responsibility is one thing, but true equipping and empowerment comes only by the Holy Spirit.

The Holy Spirit must first of all be poured out on the members of the body, imparting and calling forth spiritual gifts through each one, just as He wills. A large part of the pastoral responsibility is then to nurture and guide the body in their gifts and, in the process, to see that these same people are being enabled to nurture and guide others also. Anyone who has tried to make this happen knows that only God can do it, but, thankfully, by the power of the Holy Spirit it has already been provided for.

Paul wrote to his apprentice, Timothy, *"... The things which you have heard from me in the presence of many witnesses, these entrust to faithful men, who will be able to teach others also."*[31] The pattern for New Testament ministry is on-the-job mentoring-by-example of faithful Christians on the basis of common

---

[29] Matthew 11:30.
[30] Ephesians 4:16.
[31] II Timothy 2:2.

submission to Christ.

This release of the body into ministry is actually the longing of many a church leader, but it will not start to happen authentically until Pentecost – the infilling and overflowing of the Holy Spirit – is released into the church. The Pentecostal baptism is the experience that supplies the spiritual gifts through the people of God. It is through the gifts of the Holy Spirit that Christ so powerfully restores the ministry *of* the church *to* the church, and that is one reason why some, desperate to keep the ministry exclusively in the domain of the 'professionals', have been so resistant to the charismatic experience.

7 UNDERSTANDING THE BAPTISM IN THE HOLY SPIRIT

*"**baptisma**, baptism, consisting of the process of immersion, submersion and emergence (from bapto, to dip) ..."*

W. E. Vine[32]

When John the Baptist announced that the One coming after him was going to baptise with the Spirit and with fire, just what was he talking about? To understand the baptism with the Holy Spirit, we must first of all understand baptism.

The original Greek verb used in the New Testament was 'baptidzo', which meant to dip, immerse, or submerge. For example, it was used in ancient times of the dyeing of garments by plunging them into a container of the appropriately hued water – the fabric became completely saturated and was coloured throughout.

Many Christians, if asked whether they had been baptised with the Holy Spirit, would respond with varying degrees of uncertainty. The question, therefore, might be better asked this way: have you been filled, whelmed over and saturated with the Spirit of God? If you have, you will also have known what the first Christians experienced when it happened to them: great liberty and boldness accompanied by the fruits and gifts of the Holy Spirit.

---

[32] Vine's Expository Dictionary of Old and New Testament Words, Edited by F.F. Bruce (World Bible Publishers, 1981), *p*. 96.

A major cause for confusion regarding the baptism with the Holy Spirit has been the idea, touched upon in an earlier chapter, that the baptism is synonymous with the conversion experience, received automatically when somebody becomes a Christian. Although in an ideal world this would probably be the case, it has not been the experience of most people who have received it. In fact, the baptism with the Spirit was once commonly referred to as 'the second blessing'.

In common with millions of others, I received the baptism with the Holy Spirit some time after becoming a Christian. For the first nine months after my conversion, I increasingly struggled; in fact, I quickly despaired of ever being of any use to God. I went through the motions of going to church but, as the months rolled on, my spiritual life just seemed to ebb away.

I also came to realise that it wasn't only I who had a problem. Although I never frowned upon traditional church life, and I deeply respected those who joyfully soldiered on in church situations that were often dry, I was convinced from reading the New Testament that church ought to be a vibrant, empowering place.

As soon as I discovered the baptism in the Holy Spirit in the Book of Acts, I began praying and trusting God for it. Then one night, I asked a Christian friend to pray for me to receive it. As I sat down on a chair in his room, he laid his hand on my head and spent a short time praying. Then he turned to me and told me to start praising God with the new gift He had given me. That was when I began praising God in a language I had never heard before. Only about four or five words came at first, but I was so excited I kept saying them over and over again in case I forgot them. Like a child, I had discovered a treasure I dared not lose.

As is always the case, the gift of tongues did not come alone. 'Enraptured' would not be too dramatic a word to describe how I felt. Jesus became so much more real and personal to me. I was keenly aware of His presence. I would find myself walking along corridors singing praise songs, undeterred by the turning heads and strange looks – in pre-Christian days I would have thought nothing of wandering around singing or humming the hits of the day, so should it not be expected for a Christian to sing away naturally about God being good? The inhibition that had stifled my voice was gone as my life overflowed with joy and praise.

The most exciting effect of my new experience was that people began approaching me and asking about God. They saw something different in my life that made them curious. Once they were satisfied that I wasn't *completely* off my trolley, some would ask me what was I so happy about? Then came all the questions ... 'How can you prove there is a God?' 'Why all the suffering in the world?' 'What about all the other religions?' 'What about creation?' 'Aren't we all Christians?' But sometimes, best of all, 'How can I become a Christian?'

Over that period of time, I came to realise that, amidst all the scepticism of our supposedly post-Christian society, many people are genuinely seeking after spiritual truth. Through the local church I was now a part of, I had the joy of seeing a number of young people becoming Christians. In nine months of trying my best as a Christian I had not had the opportunities to share about Jesus that I was now finding on a daily basis. The message of Pentecost for the discouraged Christian and the demoralised church is simple: **There's more!**

Jesus said, *"You shall receive power when the Holy Spirit has come upon you."*[33] Here, He makes the purpose of the baptism with the Spirit very clear — its purpose was not to make people Christians, but to make Christians powerful.

The Day of Pentecost, according to the late renowned Bible teacher Dr Martin Lloyd Jones, was not, as some have supposed, the day the church was birthed; it was the day the now-existing church was empowered for service.

Lloyd-Jones put it this way: *"The baptism of the Holy Spirit is one of power. It was never designed to constitute the church. Its object and purpose were to give power to the church that is already constituted. It is as if our Lord was saying to them: All right, you are already my body but you must have this power in addition; so stay where you are in Jerusalem until you have received."*[34]

Thankfully, we do not have to go to Jerusalem to receive the baptism with the Holy Spirit! When Jesus told the disciples to wait in Jerusalem (Acts 1:4), what He was effectively saying was, 'There's no point embarking on your mission until you've been empowered by the Holy Spirit. Don't bother setting off in My service until you've received a strength and power greater than your own.' The same is true for us today. But troublingly, the Pentecostal baptism is no longer seen by many as essential for candidates for the ministry, let alone a requirement for every believer.

I was once amazed to be told by a learned minister that "there was only one Pentecost." I had to point out to him that five spiritual 'Pentecosts' were recorded in the Book of Acts alone. The only thing that was not repeated from Acts chapter 2 were the external physical phenomena and the calendar

---

[33] Acts 1:8.
[34] *Joy Unspeakable*, Martyn Lloyd-Jones (Kingsway Publications, 1984), *p.* 259.

date itself. Yes, there was only one glorious beginning, but what was initially experienced by the 120 was later experienced by multiplied others also. Many lesser beginnings were to follow, the vast majority of them unrecorded by history ... and they certainly didn't stop at the end of Acts chapter 28!

So, what about the other 'Pentecosts' recorded in the Book of Acts?

The second instance we have is the Samaritan believers who had *"received the word of God"* and *"been baptised in the name of the Lord Jesus.'"* Peter and John *"began laying their hands on them, and they were receiving the Holy Spirit."*[35]

The third instance, in chapter 9, verses 10 to 19, is where Saul of Tarsus experiences his personal Pentecost through the laying on of hands by a disciple called Ananias. Notice how Ananias addresses this former persecutor of the church as *"Brother"* Saul before he is filled with the Holy Spirit. Again, the baptism with the Holy Spirit comes to someone who is already converted.

Fourthly, we see our first Gentile Pentecost in the house of Cornelius in chapter 10, verses 44 to 48, where the Jewish believers were amazed to see them speaking with tongues and exalting God, just as they had themselves in the beginning.

And fifthly, in chapter 19, verses 1 to 6, the "disciples" at Ephesus who hadn't even heard of the Holy Spirit, received water baptism and then, subsequently, their Pentecostal baptism ... *"And they began speaking with tongues and prophesying ..."*[36]

The Book of Acts, according to the pattern set out by Jesus in chapter 1, verse 8, traces Pentecost from Jerusalem into Judea and Samaria, and into the Roman Empire, as we have just seen. But, in chapter 28, verse 31, the book ends abruptly and without conclusion. Why? Because the story of the Holy Spirit and the church was not over yet. We now know that it had only just begun. The power of Pentecost has still to reach *"the remotest parts of the earth"* today.

My wife has a friend who has given his life to reaching an unreached tribe in the Amazon jungle. When he eventually gets to them (they have already been many years in preparation), his mission is to live with them, befriend them, learn their language, and translate the Scriptures into their mother tongue. After the Gospel has been received, I expect these South American Indians, two thousand years down the road, will experience their own 'Day of

---

[35] Acts 8:16.
[36] Acts 19:6.

Pentecost' too!

As Peter declared at the end of his first sermon, the promise is ... *"for all who are far off, as many as the Lord our God shall call to Himself."*[37] The promise of salvation still requires apostolic empowerment today. Paul wrote to the Corinthians, *"The signs of a true apostle were performed among you with all perseverance, by signs and wonders and miracles."*[38] From the first century Mediterranean world to the Amazon rainforest to the concrete jungle and the country village, the undiluted power of Pentecost is what gives the Gospel penetration today – and we delude ourselves if we think we need it any less than the church's first generation.

Jesus predicted it all during His earthly ministry. *"He who believes in Me, as the Scripture said, 'From his innermost being shall flow rivers of living water.'"*[39] John immediately follows through by indicating that Jesus was referring here to the Holy Spirit who was yet to be given.

The baptism with the Holy Spirit is an infilling, overflowing and an enveloping with the Holy Spirit that is demonstrated by the Spirit's power and accompanied by the Spirit's gifts. It has always been that way and it will continue to be that way for as long as the task of God's last days people, the church of Jesus Christ, is to preach His gospel.

---

[37] Acts 2:39.
[38] II Corinthians 12:12.
[39] John 7:38.

8 TONGUES

"It had grammar and syntax; it had inflection and expression – and it was rather beautiful! I went on allowing these new words to come to my lips for about five minutes, then said to my friends: 'Well! That must be what you mean by "speaking in tongues" …'."

Dennis Bennett[40]

Not only was speaking in tongues the first gift that the Spirit gave to the church, but it is at the forefront of the Pentecostal revivals around the world today – a recent statistic estimated that more than one half of all evangelical Christians in the world today speak in tongues. The 11th edition of *Encyclopedia Britannica* stated that the phenomenon of tongues *"recurs in the Christian revivals of every age."*

This fact can be verified through the study of church history. Speaking in tongues was still common in the church well past the first century. It is clearly cited and endorsed by early church fathers such as Tertullian and Irenaeus. The latter, between AD161 and 180, wrote, *"… We hear many of the brethren in the church who have prophetic gifts, and who speak in all tongues through the Spirit …"*[41]

Whilst it is true that tongues did eventually begin to disappear from the church, we certainly don't have to wait until the twentieth century Pentecostal revivals to see the phenomenon cropping up again. In the Middle Ages, for

---

[40] Dennis Bennett, *Nine o'clock in the Morning* (Kingsway Publications, 1992), *p.* 37.
[41] Irenaeus, *Refutation and Overthrow of False Doctrine*.

example, many spoke in tongues in the Southern European revivals, none more notable than those from among the Waldensians whose radical return to the New Testament surely helped prepare the way for the Reformation. Then, in the sixteenth century, tongue-speaking was also known amongst the French Huguenots, who were so terribly persecuted for their evangelical faith, and later amongst groups such as the Irvingites of the nineteenth century.

And we could also cite a number of prominent individuals. The old Scots worthy, John Welsh, for example, whom friends overheard in prayer speaking *"strange words"* about his spiritual joy. Or Thomas Walsh, one of John Wesley's foremost preachers, who wrote in his diary on March 8th, 1750, *"This morning the Lord gave me a language I knew not of, raising my soul to him in a wonderful manner."* Or Mrs. Baxter, the wife of Michael Baxter who founded The Christian Herald, who in 1885 told of being in Germany and speaking in German, a language quite unfamiliar to her, for periods of up to thirty five minutes. Or Dr. F. B. Meyer who wrote after a visit to Estonia, *"... the gift of tongues is heard quite often in the meetings, especially in the villages, but also in the towns ... When they are heard, unbelievers who may be in the audience are greatly awed."*[42]

Perhaps among the most striking examples from recent centuries would be men such as D. L. Moody who was publicly heard speaking in tongues both in Britain and America, or Charles Haddon Spurgeon, the Calvinist pastor of London's Metropolitan Tabernacle in the 1800s, often referred to as the 'Prince of Preachers'. On one occasion he explained to a congregation that when he got especially happy in the Lord, *"I break forth into a kind of gibberish which I do not myself understand."*[43]

More significant than all these examples, however, is the attention which the New Testament itself gives to speaking in tongues, especially the Book of Acts. Consider again the five 'Pentecosts' we looked at in the last chapter. In chapter 2, out of 120 believers, every one spoke in tongues. Then, in Acts chapters 10 and 19, we see that both Cornelius' household and the Ephesian believers spoke in tongues on being filled with the Holy Spirit. (Little wonder Chrysostom was to write more than three hundred years later, *"Whosoever was baptised in apostolic days, he straightway spake with tongues ..."*). This leaves us with the Samaritans in chapter 8 and Saul of Tarsus in chapter 9.

In chapter 8, we read nothing of the accompanying phenomena, but we do

---

[42] These citations also appear in *Pentecostal Rays*, pp.199-203.
[43] Dr. Donald Lee Barnett and Jeffrey P. McGregor, *Speaking in Other Tongues* (Seattle: Community Chapel Publications, 1986), *p.* 252.

read that Simon the sorcerer was so impressed by what he witnessed that he naively attempted to buy the blessing. Some supernatural phenomenon had obviously occurred, and what better explanation than that which is consistent with the other Pentecostal baptisms found in Acts? Furthermore, it is clear from the writings of Augustine and other early church fathers (such as Chrysostom), that it was commonly accepted that these Samaritans spoke in tongues on receiving the baptism with the Holy Spirit.

And lastly, we have Saul of Tarsus receiving the baptism with the Spirit in chapter 9. Although we do not read that he spoke in tongues there and then, we do know from his later epistle that he spoke in tongues more than all the Corinthians[44]. It seems clear that the baptism with the Holy Spirit in the Book of Acts came with the ability to speak in other tongues.

But wait a minute, some are thinking, does Paul not say, *"All do not speak in tongues, do they?"*[45] Yes, he did, but he is clearly talking about tongues as a gift for ministry in the public gathering – he follows on immediately by saying, *"All do not interpret, do they?"* Interpreters are only required where others are listening. The subject here is not tongues *per se*, but the use of tongues in collective worship.

It would appear that the coming together of the church at Corinth was in danger of degenerating into a disorganised rabble, with numerous people exercising their 'gifts' at the same time, without much consideration for anyone else – that is why Paul had to write "The Love Chapter' (I Corinthians 13), with its strong emphasis on preferring others. The main purpose of chapters 12 to 14 of I Corinthians is not to marginalise the gifts but to regulate their public use (especially tongues and prophecy). When Paul asks, *"all do not speak in tongues, do they?"*, the context makes it very clear that he is talking about *"when you come together"*.

But speaking in tongues is unlike the other gifts mentioned in these chapters in that it also has a personal use. It should be appreciated that tongues is more than a sign gift. Even if the missionary era was over (which it obviously is not, even in so-called 'Christian' countries), God would still not withdraw the gift of tongues. Why? Because tongues is also a gift for personal edification. Paul could hardly have been clearer when he wrote, *"One who speaks in a tongue edifies himself ..."*[46]. Why would God deny the twentieth century Christian a means of personal spiritual edification that was freely available to the first

---

[44] I Corinthians 14:18.
[45] I Corinthians 12:30.
[46] I Corinthians 14:4.

century Christian?

One would think that Paul's command – *"Do not forbid to speak in tongues!"*[47] – and his exhortation – *"I wish that you all spoke in tongues"*[48] – would make the biblical position for speaking in tongues unassailable, but these are admonitions that some simply refuse to see. Tongues has been a greatly misunderstood blessing (no pun intended!).

Paul does not, as some have suggested, seek to discourage or downplay tongues in his epistle to the Corinthians; what he does seek to do is to eradicate the improper use of them in the public gathering. In chapters 12 to 14, he does not want to abolish tongues because of the excesses of some any more than he wants to abolish the sacrament of communion in chapter 11 because of the Corinthians' abuses in that area; he simply wants everything to be done in a godly manner. After telling them he is thankful that he speaks in tongues more than any of them, he goes on to say, *"However,* **in the church** *I desire to speak five words with my mind, that I may instruct others also, rather than ten thousand words in a tongue."*[49] (Emphasis mine). Some have misinterpreted this epistle by suggesting Paul seeks to downplay the charismatic gifts, when their richness in the 'charismata' is actually among the very first things he praises them for – *"I thank my God always concerning you … that you are not lacking in any gift, as you eagerly await the revelation of our Lord Jesus Christ."*[50]

Where the Corinthians went wrong was that they allowed self-centred attitudes to dictate their use of not only the spiritual gifts, but just about everything else also. One reason Paul was able to say that he spoke in tongues more than any of them may well have been that they hardly did it at all in their personal prayer lives. They probably just 'paraded it on Sundays' when, if they had been motivated by love rather than childish boasting and self-expression, they should instead have preferred to prophesy, for the *"edification and exhortation and consolation"*[51] of others. Or they could at least have accompanied their tongues with interpretation, so that the body might benefit.

The gift of tongues has been made available without discrimination to all Christians regardless of nationality, age, gender, academic privilege or historical context. If tongues are from God, then we should desire them to

---

[47] I Corinthians 14:39.
[48] I Corinthians 14:5.
[49] I Corinthians 14:19.
[50] I Corinthians 1:4, 7.
[51] I Corinthians 14:3.

be exercised privately and in the church.

Tongues are a wonderful blessing from the Holy Spirit, a privilege which, according to I Corinthians chapter 14, may be used or not used at will. Yes, they may serve as a sign to unbelievers, but they are much more than that. Tongues are a glorious means of expressing the inexpressible praises of God, vitalising our personal prayer lives and mysteriously unlocking many of God's blessings.

In the early months of my Christian life, I recall being taught at a Navigators Bible study: *the answer to misuse is not disuse but proper use*. There are few better biblical examples of the correct application of this principle than in the area of speaking in tongues. If God, in His wisdom and grace, has decided to give us tongues, then we ought to humbly and gratefully receive them, and use them at every appropriate opportunity.

9 PROPHECY

"'And it shall be in the last days,' God says, 'that I will pour forth of My Spirit upon all mankind; and your sons and your daughters shall prophecy, and your young men shall see visions, and your old men shall dream dreams; even upon My bondslaves, both men and women, I will in those days pour forth of My Spirit and they shall prophesy.'"

The Acts of the Apostles[52]

In 1981, Alex Gillies, then pastor of the Glasgow Christian Fellowship, stood before about twenty Christians at a prayer gathering in Glasgow city centre, and told them of a vision he had just seen … a fleet of ships sailing from Britain towards South America, an ensuing naval battle, vessels being sunk, and lives lost, then a large white ship arriving, and finally the British flag being hoisted. He told the Christians gathered that they needed to pray.

After the meeting Alex was reprimanded by one of the leaders of the church for his over-the-top behaviour! Yet he was convinced that what he had seen was real and responded that if none of this came to pass within the next twelve months, then he would retract and apologise for what he had done. He had at that time never heard of the Falkland Isles, but he learned all about them nine months later during a visit to Canada when the Falklands War exploded across the world media.

On his return home he was inundated with telephone calls, not to ask how

---

[52] Acts 2:17-18; Joel 2:28-29.

his ministry trip to Canada had gone, but to express astonishment at the fulfilment of the prophecy. *"What's going to happen now?"*, one caller asked him. *"A large white ship is going to enter the scene and the British flag is going to be raised,"* he replied. Days later, the lead story was that the QE2 had been requisitioned by the UK Government and was sailing south with 3,000 troops aboard. The rest of the episode is now well documented history.

This, of course, is an unusually dramatic incidence of the gift of prophecy, but it bears similarity to the revelation of a coming famine given to Agabus in Antioch, recorded in Acts chapter 11, and serves to illustrate once more that the experiences of first century Christianity should still be expected in our churches today. Experiences like that of Agabus, and indeed that of Alex Gillies, are not by nature everyday occurrences of the prophetic gift. Less spectacular prophetic utterances appear to have been commonplace in the New Testament.

As we have already touched on, a popular misinterpretation of I Corinthians, chapters 12 to 14, is that Paul is saying we ought to desire to walk in love rather than seeking after the gifts. That is most definitely *not* what he is saying. What he is very clearly teaching is that our exercising of the gifts should be ruled by love. We are not expected to choose between a Christ-like nature and the charismatic gifts; we are expected to have both, with the former motivating and governing the latter.

Immediately after concluding the 'Love Chapter' (I Corinthians 13), Paul continues, *"Pursue love, yet earnestly desire spiritual gifts, but especially that you may prophesy."*[53] When it comes to public worship, prophecy is to be preferred to tongues, simply because *"one who speaks in a tongue edifies himself; but one who prophesies edifies the church."*[54] If love is the motivating factor, and love seeks the benefit of others before self, then, in the public gathering, prophecy is more appropriate than tongues – unless, of course, the tongues are interpreted so that *all* might be enlightened.

Like tongues, prophecy appears to have commonly accompanied the baptism with the Holy Spirit. When Peter stood up on the Day of Pentecost to give explanation to what was happening, he said it was the fulfilment of what had been foretold by the prophet Joel ... *"'And it shall be in the last days,' God says, 'That I will pour forth of My Spirit on all mankind; and your sons and your daughters shall prophesy, and your young men shall see visions, and your old men shall dream dreams; even upon my bondslaves, both men and women, I will in those days pour forth of My*

---

[53] I Corinthians 14:1.
[54] I Corinthians 14:4.

Spirit, and they shall prophesy'."[55]

Prophesying was a result of the outpouring of the Holy Spirit. Young and old, male and female, slave and free – if you could be filled with the Holy Spirit, then you could prophesy. When the Holy Spirit is poured out, He elevates the marginalised and belittled ... the 'under-aged', the 'over-aged', and the overlooked.

The latter issue, women in ministry, was initially an area of heated debate in more conservative denominations when the Holy Spirit began to sweep through the church of the twentieth century. And yet women prophesying was clearly expected in the New Testament. Philip the evangelist *"had four virgin daughters who were prophetesses."*[56] Then there was Paul's instruction to the Corinthian women to have their heads covered *"while praying or prophesying."*[57] Shortly after I first became a Christian, I remember such a song and dance being made in one church about the issue of women wearing head-coverings, and yet no one seemed to be asking, *'Why are our women not praying and prophesying in church?'!* The Bible is there as a guide to live by, not as a tool to extinguish life; it never enslaves, always liberates (John 8:31-32).

The Holy Spirit is a great equaliser, and when He comes upon the church, He is liable to speak prophetically through anyone, just as He wills. *"For you can all prophesy one by one, so that all may learn and all may be exhorted,"*[58] Paul wrote to the Corinthians.

Earlier in the same chapter, Paul wrote, *"... If all prophesy and an unbeliever or an ungifted man enters, he is convicted by all, he is called to account by all; the secrets of his heart are disclosed; and so he will fall on his face and worship God, declaring that God is certainly among you."*[59] Special things are to be expected in a church that experiences the gift of prophecy!

Perhaps the most significant aspect of Joel's prophecy for us, however, is the time context of its application – *"the last days."* Bible scholars agree that the last days began at Pentecost and, since we are obviously not yet at the end of the age, we are still in living in the last days today; *"the last days"* is simply the age of the church. The gift of prophecy, as with the Pentecostal baptism, was not an *early* church blessing, but a *church* blessing, and it will remain available

---

[55] Acts 2:17-18.
[56] Acts 21:9.
[57] I Corinthians 11:5.
[58] I Corinthians 14:31.
[59] I Corinthians 14:24-25.

until such time as Jesus Christ Himself calls an end to the church age.

We have seen that the purpose of prophecy is *"to speak to men for their edification and exhortation and consolation."*[60] But prophecy, like tongues, has also been greatly misunderstood. Some have reasoned, as they did regarding tongues and other gifts, that since we now have the New Testament, we no longer need another source of revelation. This is based upon a misunderstanding of the nature of the gift of prophecy in the New Testament.

Donald Gee, the early twentieth century Pentecostal pioneer, deals with this misunderstanding by pointing out that *"such an argument ... assumes that in the early church, utterances through these gifts had all the authority of the Scriptures, but the New Testament utterly disproves such an idea. The early church is consistently found always appealing to the Scriptures of the Old Testament (never to their own 'prophets' be it noted), for support for all doctrine and final settlement in every dispute. Acts 2:16; 15:15; 26:22. The 'prophecy of Scripture' (II Peter 1:20) provided a totally different level of authority to the spiritual gifts among them, and it does so still."*[61]

If the simple New Testament gift of prophecy was ever intended to carry the same authority as Scripture, then what became of the prophecies of the four daughters of Philip the evangelist, or the prophetic utterances of the believers at Ephesus, or, for that matter, those of the church at Corinth? Why are they not contained in our New Testaments? Simply because, as Gee pointed out, the gift of prophecy never did and still does not carry the same weight as Scripture. The gift of prophecy is no more a rival to the authority of Scripture today than it was when it was exercised in the New Testament; it is simply a revealing of God's will by the inspiration of the Holy Spirit that is specific, timely and relevant to a given situation, and above all never at discord with the general counsel of Scripture.

Scripture is infallible; prophetic utterances are not. George Jeffreys, one of the pioneers of twentieth century Pentecostalism in Britain, wrote, *"Every prophetical utterance should be judged, and if there is the least suggestion of guidance in any prophecy, the persons concerned should feel intuitively within whether they ought to obey, and only contemplate action after consulting those who are in a position to judge without prejudice."*[62] This echoes the instruction of Paul to the Corinthians to *"let two or three prophets speak, and let the others pass judgement."*[63] Scripture, on the other

---

[60] I Corinthians 14:3.
[61] *Concerning Spiritual Gifts;* Donald Gee.
[62] George Jeffreys, *Pentecostal Rays* (Elim Publishing Company, 1933); *p.* 191.
[63] I Corinthians 14:29.

hand, is not to be judged, but obeyed.

However, this is not to say that prophecy should be taken lightly. The gift prophecy affects people's lives and ought to be exercised with wisdom and a sense of responsibility. In Paul's first letter to Timothy, he urges his disciple, *"Do not neglect the spiritual gift within you, which was bestowed upon you through prophetic utterance through the laying on of hands by the presbytery."*[64] Here is a case where a prophecy, delivered by church leadership, had given Timothy a clear commission, apparently even specifying a certain gift which would become evident in his ministry ... a gift for which Paul now appeared to be holding Timothy accountable! The gift of prophecy had not only united them in the same venture, but also bound them in the same responsibility.

As we have seen, because prophecy is subject to the fallibility of human vessels, it must also be tested. If any prophecy is inconsistent with the Bible's teachings, then it is to be rejected. But to steer clear of a gift that Christ has given to the church for fear that it might be misused is to mislead. The solution, again, to misuse is not disuse but proper use. This means not only drawing from the wisdom and advice of experienced Christians, but also continuing to grow in the full counsel of Scripture. Prophecy, like all the other gifts, does not diminish our reliance on Scripture; quite the contrary, it increases it.

The purpose of the gift of prophecy, it cannot be over-stressed, is simply to *"edify, exhort and comfort."*[65] Where the genuine New Testament gift of prophecy is exercised, the result is that Christians will be further strengthened, encouraged and established in the faith – there cannot be anything more biblical.

How thankful the believers of the New Testament must have been when, faced with the coming onslaught of persecution, a Spirit-filled believer would stand up in the midst of the church and declare that God would not desert them in their hour of need.

Even though my personal trials have been extremely mild compared to those of New Testament believers, I thank God for the times when, faced with trials and discouragements, the prophetic gift has come through a faithful Christian shedding the light of God's word on my situation. These words of encouragement have often been accompanied by biblical metaphor or quotation, if they were not simply timely quotations from Scripture itself. At

---

[64] I Timothy 4:14.
[65] I Corinthians 14:3.

the very least, they directed me back to the Scriptures looking for more of the same! How can such a gift do anything but strengthen and inspire our churches in the purposes of God? How could a Christian be anything other than grateful that the gift of prophecy is still available to the church, God's 'last days' people!

Long before Joel predicted the outpouring of the Holy Spirit and the gift of prophecy, and even longer before Paul realised that all could prophesy in turn, Moses had wished *"that all the Lord's people were prophets, that the Lord would put His Spirit upon them!"*[66] We are living in days that Moses would have rejoiced to see (and maybe did), days of the outpouring of the Holy Spirit *"on all flesh"*: the age of the church!

When Jesus Christ returns, may He find a people who are faithful and faith-filled in exercising *all* the gifts with which He has seen necessary to endow His church. *"Pursue love, yet desire earnestly spiritual gifts, but especially that you may prophesy!"*[67]

---

[66] Numbers 11:29.
[67] I Corinthians 14:1.

10 PENTECOST AND THE LOCAL CHURCH

"There are spiritual truths I will never grasp and Christian standards I will never attain except as I share in community with other believers – and this is God's plan ... Gifts must be seen not as spiritual fringe benefits but as completely central to the life, experience and functioning of the Christian community."

Howard A. Snyder[68]

The gifts need the church every bit as much as the church needs the gifts. Biblically formed local churches are essential if the workings of the Holy Spirit are going to have an enduring influence on the world around us. Thankfully the New Testament gives us some clear patterns and principles for healthy church life.

Although *community* was a basic mark of the early church, the individualism of our modern western society has often made genuine, life-sharing fellowship very difficult. As with other justified shortcomings, our individualism has turned the ability 'to stand alone' into a mark of spirituality. Any sense of dependence upon others must therefore be a sign of weakness. Where this individualism has isolated Christians from one another, it has had a crippling effect on the church, which is described in the New Testament as the *body* of Christ.

---

[68] Howard A. Snyder, *The Community of The King* (Inter-Varsity Press, 1977), *pp*. 75-76.

Somewhere along the way, probably by gradual process, the early church's vital sense of dependency upon God dropped out of organised Christianity. It follows without saying that if Christians could manage to get along without relying too heavily upon God, then any sense of inter-dependence with fellow Christians would seem almost ridiculous! We have come a long way from the almost communal lifestyle of the first church.

I remember in my early Christian experience an almost heroic feeling some of us had about being members of an 'independent' Christian fellowship! That sense of 'authenticity', however, began to erode as 'Independent' evolved into an official category in the church listings amongst the denominations! But why not? After all, what else is a denomination but an independent church that got big?

Where individualism reigns, Christians become isolated units within isolated churches within isolated denominations, in a world that idealises independence. Whatever happened to *"the eye cannot say to the hand, 'I have no need of you' ..."*[69]?

Jesus said, *"I will build My **church**; and the gates of Hades shall not overpower it."*[70] (Emphasis mine.) He did not say that He would create a race of spiritual 'supermen', but rather an entity of mutually dependent component parts which He called His church, and He has fashioned this organism, as a *body*, in such a way that each part can only operate effectively out of its union with the whole. The church is a family, a community that Christ has sanctioned to represent Him on earth, and our strength is no greater than our depth of relationship and identity with one another.

Jesus' brief earthly ministry was twin-pronged: on one hand He was reaching out to a lost world, whilst at the same time taking His disciples through a course of training, preparing and grooming them for service within His church. He did this by calling them into relationship with Him and growing in their relationship with Him also meant growing in their relationship with one another.

The importance of *relationship* was crucial to Jesus; He knew that His followers would never be stronger individually than they were collectively. In Mark's Gospel we read, *"... He appointed twelve, **that they might be with Him**, and that He might send them out to preach ..."*[71] (Emphasis mine.) Notice the

---

[69] I Corinthians 12:21.
[70] Matthew 16:18.
[71] Mark 3:14.

order: relationship first; ministry second. The principle is not ministry-based relationships, but relationship-based ministry. Christ has designed it that ministry should develop out of and be safeguarded by relationships. If any body of Christians starts to lose its way, or if, more seriously, conflict should emerge, and there is no effective network of relationships through which direction can be brought and peace restored, then the "gates of Hades" shall certainly overpower it.

It is all too apparent that being part of a denomination is in itself no safeguard against schism and unrest. Only meaningful relationships will do: Christ-centred relationships out of which, as they mature, evolves real accountability on the basis of biblical truth, proven loyalty, a servant attitude, and the various callings evident in people's lives. Mature relationships are marked by responsibility, and that is why some, under the misnomer of freedom, have found it easier to go the way of independence. Such 'freedom' is always short-lived.

Relationship, loyalty, accountability ... What has all this got to do with Pentecost and the gifts of the Holy Spirit? The trouble is that some would seriously ask that question. If we are going to start getting involved with the charismatic gifts and ministering to others in the power of the Spirit, *then*, more than ever before, we need to have in place all the checks and balances that Christ has given to His body. For his or her own protection as well as for the safety of others, the Spirit-filled believer who is exercising spiritual gifts must operate out of a real, meaningful relationship with a local body of believers.

The power of Pentecost is not for self-styled mavericks or lone rangers who wander the country, answerable to no one except 'the Lord' (that is, themselves!). Nor is it for those who drift endlessly from one church to the next, ever seeking the perfect home, never settled, unplantable and therefore ungrowable. Such people, sometimes wounded in past dysfunctional relationships, have failed to see that it is for our protection that God has designed that we be firmly planted in a local church, harnessed by relationships of love, loyalty and mutual responsibility.

When the Ephesians were instructed to *"submit to one another out of reverence for Christ"*[72], they were effectively being told that the maturity of their relationship to Jesus Christ was measurable by their ability to live and work with His people. We cannot touch Jesus without touching His body. The

---

[72] Ephesians 5:21.

perfect model of unity was found in Jesus' own prayer when He longed *"that they might be one, even as We are."*[73] Christ's desire for His people is that we be attached to and functioning with one another, just as He was with the Father for the duration of His own earthly ministry.

In reading through the Gospels, especially John's, we very quickly find that Jesus did not come to earth to 'do his own thing'. In an age when so much has beeen made, even in the church, of 'discovering your true self', it is worth considering that Jesus did not embark upon His ministry as a quest for self-realisation. Yes, He found fulfilment through His ministry, but His ministry found its consummation through the cross, the ultimate denial of self. He did not come to 'find' Himself – He came to forfeit self and find us! He did not derive His fulfilment from the exercising of spiritual gifts but from the knowledge of how these gifts were serving others, and washing His disciples' feet was no doubt as meaningful to Him as preaching the Sermon on the Mount.

Consequently, Jesus has not given His gifts to the church as a means of self-fulfilment, although there is nothing on earth more rewarding than the consciousness of being used by God. The purpose of the gifts is not *self*-expression but *Christ*-expression. Our meaning in life is to be found in the service of Jesus Christ and of His people, and that will at times require us to make room for the gifts of others for the good of the whole. This is precisely what Paul was calling for in I Corinthians chapter 14.

The New Testament church is characterised by relationships of love and respect, trust and loyalty, faithfulness and accountability, to both Christ and His people. It is only in and out of such a culture that the gifts of the Spirit will flourish for long. Christians and churches wilt in isolation, and many ministries-in-the-making have foundered needlessly when the wisdom and experience of Christians of spiritual stature could easily have saved the day. Even in times of crisis, it would surprise many just how near at hand such spiritual help usually is.

---

[73] John 17:11.

11 PREPARING FOR PENTECOST

"The Holy Spirit of God ... This is our need tonight. Will God give to us what He gave to them? Yes! yes! Yes! What are the conditions? God gives all to those who give Him their all."[74]

C. T. Studd

American evangelist T. L. Osborn once shocked a Christian television audience by declaring that he believed in reincarnation. When asked to explain, he said that Jesus Christ became incarnate 2000 years ago; but then, after He died, rose from the dead and ascended to be with the Father, He sent the Spirit to dwell in the church, thus 're-incarnating' Himself in His followers! "Yes, I believe in reincarnation," he said, "I believe in the 'reincarnation' of 'Christ in you', the church, by the Holy Spirit! I believe in the body of Christ!"

The new birth is the experience through which the Jesus of the gospels, by the Holy Spirit, comes to dwell within those who become His followers. Because of this wonderful truth, every Christian has tremendous potential to become His minister. The purpose of the baptism with the Holy Spirit is to take a believer and to so breathe upon him that he becomes effective in passing his experience of Jesus on to others. The baptism with the Spirit, like the new birth, is more than a doctrine; it is an experience.

So, how can we experience the baptism with the Spirit? Firstly, we must be

---

[74] John T. Erskine, *Millionaire for God* (Lutterworth Press, 1968), *p.* 91.

born again. The person who has not been converted to Christ is not yet a candidate for the baptism with the Holy Spirit. If you are unsure about your salvation, ask yourself the two 'diagnostic questions' used so effectively by *Evangelism Explosion*.

Firstly, *if I were to die right now, do I know for sure that I would go to heaven?* If you are unsure, then ask yourself the second question: *if I were to stand before God, and He were to ask me, 'Why should I let you into heaven?', what would my answer be?* If your response is that you're not really sure, or that you've tried to be a good person, or something similar to that, then ask yourself one final question: *if I could get to heaven by being a good person, then why did Christ have to die on the cross?*

If you are trusting in your own efforts to get to heaven, then that is self-righteousness! The Bible says that *"all have sinned and fall short of the glory of God"*[75], and that *"there is none righteous, not even one"*[76]. Man cannot save himself by his own, strivings any more than he can lift himself off the ground by his own shoelaces. We need a Saviour, and that is why Jesus came into the world.

"For God so loved the world, that He gave His only begotten Son, that whoever believes in Him should not perish, but have eternal life"[77]. Trusting in Jesus is the only way. To trust in our own or somebody else's efforts is to fail to understand Christ's whole purpose in coming into this world, which was to save a people who were unable to save themselves. To trust in our own efforts is in effect to say that His death on the cross was unnecessary. Every true Christian has found that good works are a *result* of salvation, not a *means* of it. No religious code can save us, whether it be Islamic, Buddhist, or Christian ritual – only Jesus Christ can save.

To become a Christian is not only to repent of our sin, but also to cease depending on our own efforts as a means of justification, and to trust in and confess Jesus Christ as our personal Saviour and Lord. Paul wrote that, *"if you confess with your mouth Jesus as Lord, and believe in your heart that God raised Him from the dead, you shall be saved ..."*[78]

Our assurance of salvation does not depend on an emotional feeling, or even on becoming a better person (although this does happen His as we depend on is strength), but rather on God's faithfulness to the promises of His Word. When we truly grasp that our salvation rests upon His provision and not on

---

[75] Romans 3:10.
[76] Romans 3:23.
[77] John 3:16.
[78] Romans 10:9.

our performance, we will begin to see a radical improvement in our performance!

The second thing we need to consider in preparing to receive the baptism with the Holy Spirit is, *Why* do we want it? As we have seen, Jesus was very clear about why He provided it: *"... You shall receive power when the Holy Spirit has come upon you; and you shall be My witnesses both in Jerusalem, and in all Judea and Samaria, and even to the remotest part of the earth."*[79] To ask for the baptism with the Spirit is to ask to be made an effective witness for Jesus Christ, and our goal is to play our part in reaching everyone, from next door to the ends of the earth, with His gospel.

Probably just about every wrong motive imaginable was at work in Simon the Sorcerer when he sought the Spirit's empowerment in Acts chapter 8. He was infatuated with the supernatural – it was also his means of income! – and saw this baptism with the Spirit as a means of career advancement. But the baptism with the Spirit is a means to a self-less end, the fulfilling of Christ's Great Commission to preach His gospel to all creation. It is never an end in itself.

Thirdly, is my relationship with God and with other people being hindered by unconfessed sin in my life? To *walk in the light* does not mean living in sinless perfection, simply that we are not hiding sin or stubbornly resisting the Spirit's correction but walking in openness and correctability before God. Ananias and Sapphira were to find out, at the cost of their lives in Acts chapter 5, that it is a dangerous thing to seek to get involved in the work of the Spirit and not walk in the light at the same time.

I once thought that the baptism is God's instrument in enabling Christians to live a holy life. But it is clear from the Day of Pentecost that the baptism with the Spirit came to a people who were not so much desperate to attain to 'holiness' as despairing of their own ability ever to achieve it, much less serve their Saviour in power of the Holy Spirit. They were not perfect – far from it, they were now completely humbled by their own imperfection. Pentecost came to a body of believers who were utterly convinced of their need for something more than they were able to produce themselves. They did not have to attain a humanly impossible to receive God's empowerment, just thoroughly convicted of their personal need.

John explains very clearly what it means to walk in the light ... *"... If we walk in the light as He Himself is in the light, we have fellowship with one another, and the*

---

[79] Acts 1:8.

blood of Jesus His Son cleanses us from all sin. If we say that we have no sin, we are deceiving ourselves, and the truth is not in us. If we confess our sins, He is faithful and righteous to forgive us our sins and to cleanse us from all unrighteousness."[80]

Fourthly, how much do I want to receive it? The people who received from Jesus in the Bible were invariably desperate people. You cannot come to receive the baptism with the attitude, 'Oh, I think that would be good. If God means for me to have it, then I'm sure it will come.' No! The attitude must be, 'I cannot go on without it!' When you're that desperate, you won't have to wait long. Jesus said, *"Blessed are those who hunger and thirst for righteousness, for they shall be satisfied."*[81]

Having said all this, there need not be any delay between conversion and baptism with the Spirit. The variable factor is not God, but our response to His promise. It is God, not we, who exercises patience! We are wondering if God is ready when, in actual fact, He is waiting for *us* to be ready! How *hungry* are we? How *much* do we want it?

And fifthly, we should count the cost. We must realise that not everyone is going to respond to us positively, and some may even react with hostility. The Acts of the Apostles is not only the book of power and miracles; it is also the book of prisons and martyrdom. Power and persecution go hand-in-hand in the New Testament. In the Book of Acts, we find Stephen, *"full of grace and power, ... performing great wonders and signs among the people"*[82]. But in the very next chapter, *"they went on stoning Stephen as he called upon the Lord and said, 'Lord Jesus, receive my Spirit.'"*[83]

As we count the cost, however, we can be confident that the blessing far outweighs the pain. *"Momentary, light affliction,"* Paul declared, *"is producing for us an eternal weight of glory far beyond all comparison."*[84] The fullness of the Spirit elevates Christians above persecutions. Whether it was Stephen's face shining like that of an angel while awaiting execution for blasphemy, or Silas and Paul singing praises to God in a Philippian jail, the Holy Spirit has a way of lifting the Christian's vision beyond the temporal trials of life and using these very afflictions to produce even more joy.

But above all, we should know that it pleases God to baptise us with His Holy Spirit. When the Holy Spirit descended upon Jesus after His baptism in

---

[80] 1 John 1:7-9.
[81] Matthew 5:6.
[82] Acts 6:8.
[83] Acts 7:59.
[84] II Corinthians 4:17.

the Jordan, a voice came out of heaven saying, *"This is My beloved Son, in whom I am well-pleased."*[85] There can be few things more pleasing to God than to see us seeking to serve Him as Jesus' witnesses. That is a task for which we need more than enthusiastic commitment, and for which He is more than glad to empower us with the Holy Spirit.

---

[85] Matthew 3:17.

12 EXPERIENCING PENTECOST

"How do you pray for this blessing? You plead the promises."

D. Martyn Lloyd-Jones[86]

"Ask, and it shall be given to you; seek, and you shall find; knock, and it shall be opened to you. For everyone who asks, receives; and he who seeks, finds; and to him who knocks, it shall be opened."[87]

These words in Luke's gospel are among the best-known prayer promises in the Bible. However, not too many people are familiar with how Jesus goes on to apply them ... *"Now suppose one of you fathers is asked by his son for a fish; he will not give him a snake instead of a fish, will he? Or if he is asked for an egg, he will not give him a scorpion, will he? If you then, being evil, know how to give good gifts to your children, how much more shall your heavenly Father give the **Holy Spirit** to those who ask Him?"*[88] (Emphasis mine.)

So, Jesus was saying that if we ask, seek and knock, then the Holy Spirit will be given to us. To receive the baptism with the Holy Spirit, we simply have to ask our heavenly Father with the same confident expectation that a child has with an earthly parent. We can pray with faith when we are secure in

---

[86] D. Martyn Lloyd-Jones, *Joy Unspeakable* (Kingsway Publications, 1984), *p.* 208.
[87] Luke 11:9-10.
[88] Luke 11:11-13.

our relationship with Him, and when we know by His word that it is His will to give us the thing for which we are asking.

If our faith is weak, it is often because we have not been nourishing it with the promises of God's word – Paul wrote that *"faith comes from hearing, and hearing by the word of Christ."*[89] So, as we pray, it is always helpful to re-examine the Scriptures, the revealed will of God for our lives. We will then have the confidence that John wrote of: *"If we ask anything according to His will, he hears us. And if we know that He hears us in whatever we ask, we know that we have the requests which we have asked from Him."*[90]

Let's examine some of the biblical promises relating to the baptism with the Holy Spirit. At the commencement of Jesus' ministry, the gospel-writer Luke records that John the Baptist told the people, *"… One is coming who is mightier than I, and I am not fit to untie the thong of His sandals; He will baptize you with the Holy Spirit and with fire."*[91] Before Jesus even began His ministry, He was introduced by John the Baptist as the Baptiser in the Holy Spirit.

The provision of the Holy Spirit is a thread that runs through Luke's writings. In chapter 3, on Jesus' own baptism in the Jordan, the Holy Spirit descends upon Him. Then in chapter 4, Jesus goes on to quote Isaiah the prophet: *"The Spirit of the Lord is upon Me, because He anointed Me to preach the gospel to the poor. He has sent Me to proclaim release to the captives, and recovery of sight to the blind, to set free those who are downtrodden …"*[92]

Although Jesus was divine, God in the flesh, we see from such passages that He fulfilled His earthly ministry as a man baptised with the Holy Spirit. Just think about it … Emmanuel, God with us, dwelt on earth for thirty years, but we read of no sermons, no miracles, no conversions, until after He was baptised with water and the Holy Spirit. That is precisely why He was able to expect His disciples to continue His ministry after He left – they did not have to be divine to do it, simply men empowered by the same Holy Spirit who anointed Jesus for ministry.

---

[89] Romans 10:17.
[90] I John 5:14-15.
[91] Luke 3:16.
[92] Luke 4:18.

"He who believes in Me," Jesus promised, *"the works that I do shall he do also; and greater works than these shall he do; because I go to the Father."*[93] And what did He do when He went to the Father? He sent the Holy Spirit to enable believers (not just apostles or evangelists, but "the one who believes") to continue His works on earth. *"As the Father has sent Me,"* He told them before He left, *"I also send you."*[94]

But when Jesus delegates a task to His workers, He also supplies the resources necessary to carry it out. Luke ends his gospel by quoting Jesus instructing His disciples to wait for the baptism in the Holy Spirit before embarking on their commission .... *"And behold, I am sending forth the promise of My Father upon you; but you are to stay in the city until you are clothed with power from on high."*[95] Then, at the beginning of Acts, Luke continues the same narrative by recapping on Christ's command to *"wait for what the Father had promised."*[96]

What must be stressed is this: When the baptism in the Holy Spirit came, it came to a people who were already well primed and prepared by numerous promises of Jesus. They expected it. They anticipated it. They were left in no doubt that their task would be futile without it, and they were fully focused on each personally receiving it. The same ought to be the case for every Christian seeking the baptism with the Spirit today. This is why we need to prepare ourselves by studying the promises of Scripture concerning it.

When we pray to receive the baptism with the Holy Spirit, we should consider the promises as having been spoken to us personally. We must not be afraid that we are going to receive anything that is not from God. If my child asks me for an egg, will I give him a scorpion? Of course not. We likewise must trust our heavenly Father.

Whether you receive the baptism through the laying on of hands or without any human agency is not of great significance – what is important is *that* you receive it, and that you receive it in the knowledge that Jesus Christ Himself

---

[93] John 14:12.
[94] John 20:21.
[95] Luke 24:49.
[96] Acts 1:4.

is your Baptiser.

When you ask, expect to receive. Expect to speak in tongues and to prophesy. Expect to lay hands on the sick, and for them to recover. Remember that the Holy Spirit will not bypass the human will. When the utterance comes, we must still speak in faith. When the urge comes to pray for the sick, we still must step out and offer prayer.

I have known of rare cases when people seeking the baptism with the Spirit have woken up in the middle of the night speaking in tongues or were suddenly caught up and 'carried along' by the Holy Spirit, but these have been exceptions. Once we have learned what the will of God is, we must prepare our hearts and make the decision to receive, and He will supply the power. In ourselves we do not have the power, but neither will He make our decisions for us. Faith is acting on the promises of God's word, and when we act in faith, He fills our actions.

Someone speaking in tongues does not normally have any idea what he is saying. Paul wrote, *"... If I pray in a tongue, my spirit prays, but my mind is unfruitful."*[97] He does, however, know one thing: his heavenly Father has not given him a snake or a scorpion.

'But how will I know that it's not me doing it?" Well, it *is* you doing it! – by the inspiration of the Holy Spirit. On the Day of Pentecost, we read, *"And they were all filled with the Holy Spirit and began to speak with other tongues, as the Spirit was giving them utterance."*[98] They did the speaking; the Holy Spirit gave the utterance. As you speak in tongues, you know – not intellectually, but spiritually – that you have received something marvellous from God.

The baptism in the Holy Spirit introduces us to a learning experience in receiving, becoming secure in, and growing in the blessings of God. As we learn to exercise the gifts of the Spirit by faith, we start to see great blessing in the lives of ourselves and others. And as we remain in close communion with Jesus, through the Word, prayer, and the fellowship of His people, we will find that a whole new dimension of Christian living has just begun.

---

[97] I Corinthians 14:14.
[98] Acts 2:4.

13 BEYOND PENTECOST

"The supreme task of every believer is worldwide soulwinning - and that is the true purpose of Pentecost."

T. L. Osborn[99]

The great goal of the church is the fulfilment of Jesus' last command: *"Go into all the world and preach the gospel to all creation."*[100] The baptism in the Holy Spirit is the church's only empowerment towards that goal. But the empowerment is not an end in itself; it is a means to an end. The Book of Acts did not end with Pentecost; it began with it.

The Pentecostal baptism is only an initiation which provides no guarantee that we are going to go on and live Spirit-filled lives for the remainder of our time on earth. Many great challenges lie ahead, for which we will need to be repeatedly filled with the Holy Spirit. It was the evangelist D. L. Moody who said that we need to be continually filled with the Holy Spirit … because we 'leak'!

The Holy Spirit was not sent to create highly charged Christian gatherings, but as an introduction to a whole new way of life. The goal of the fulness of the Spirit is not to put on a spectacle on Sunday mornings, only to be

---

[99] T. L. Osborn, *The Purpose of Pentecost* (Osborn Foundation, 1963), *p.* 113.
[100] Mark 16:15.

hidden from view until next time – the purpose is to take us 'into all the world.'

Neither is the Holy Spirit a personal 'Genie in the Lamp' that we can conjure up in moments of need. He comes on God's terms, not ours, to lead us into His higher purposes. When the believers in Acts received the baptism with the Holy Spirit, their very lives became expendable for the sake of the gospel.

Pentecost is much more than a place of great blessing; it is fuel for the journey and tools for the task. Because the Pentecostal experience is so wonderful, the temptation for the church is to let it go no further than an exciting bless-me time for the gathered event. But the Holy Spirit will not be commandeered for an institutional agenda, because His power is not ultimately intended for us – it is for a whole world out there that has not yet tasted Christ. To receive the baptism in the Holy Spirit is to be equipped for a whole new way of life that is outward-looking and missional, and to surrender ourselves to God for full-time service.

Like the first believers, experiencing 'Pentecost' will find us instantly in situations which demand the demonstration of God's power. And it will not take too long serving Jesus in our places of work and learning, in our families and neighbourhoods, where challenges threaten to drain us and overcome us again. It is then that we realise the baptism with the Spirit was not a once-and-forever experience … and we need to be refilled constantly!

In Acts chapter 2, the disciples were filled with the Holy Spirit and experienced great liberty and boldness. But then, two chapters later, after Peter and John were released from prison, we find the believers once again joined together in prayer, just as they had been in the beginning, *"and when they had prayed, the place where they had gathered together was shaken, and they were all filled with the Holy Spirit, and began to speak the word of God with boldness."*[101]

But wait a minute. Had they not already been filled with the Holy Spirit? Yes – that is precisely the point. Every day is a new day, and we can never rest on the strength of yesterday's experience. God has not called us to an experience, but to a way of life. Believers who had been filled with the Holy

---

[101] Acts 4:31.

Spirit in Acts chapter 2 were once again being filled with the Holy Spirit in chapter 4.

Dotted around our country today are 'Charismatic' and 'Pentecostal' churches where nobody speaks in tongues, prophesies, prays for the sick or witnesses with boldness anymore. The Spirit-filled life is not about joining an appropriately tagged local church. It is a day-to-day experience, not a denomination.

I had a very special friend called Peter Nicolson who passed away a number of years ago at the age of 90, having lived the final 25 years of his life as a Spirit-filled believer in a Highland Presbyterian church. I often recall the times when we prayed together, and the radiance of his face as he would passionately declare, *"The Lord is coming back soon!"* Though he stood out as different, he carried too much sincerity and personal authority to be regarded as odd, as he stamped his feet while singing the Psalms and urged the preacher on from the pew. And when he was invited to pray, everybody knew that God was present.

What we are talking about is something much greater than denominations or churches 'with a name'. This is something which is to be found wherever Christians gathered and go in the name of Jesus. It is about the undeniable expression of God the Holy Spirit. And this can happen anywhere. Moves of the Holy Spirit have historically produced new churches, but they have also – perhaps even more remarkably – revived old ones. The extent to which Christians and churches are willing to be awakened and reformed is the measure of how ready they are for Pentecost.

We must not see the moment we are filled with the Holy Spirit as an apex of our Christian experience, but rather an ignition for a Spirit-empowered journey, a walk that has just begun. Pentecostal-charismatic churches can be just as susceptible to dryness and stagnation as any other. I have been a part of many 'charismatic' worship services where we have just gone through the motions … two or three exuberant praise songs, one or two slower worshipful ones, announcements, sermon, closing chorus and prayer, and that's it until next week, folks! Most gathered would turn up their noses at the thought of a formal 'order of service.' Contemporary, well-honed, warm, well-attended services … while the trajectory of the world outside remains unchanged.

EMPOWERED: THE BAPTISM IN THE HOLY SPIRIT

I once heard someone suggest our strapline ought to be, *Change is here to stay!* Always growing, continually challenged, constantly breaking new ground, facing every day with a fresh sense of dependence upon the Holy Spirit. Not relying upon something that happened in the past, forever harping back to the blessings of yesteryear, though occasionally inspired by them. We may have had wonderful experiences, but fossils are found where there once was life. If these surviving 'fossils' serve any purpose, it is to fuel the fire that releases the same newness now as then.

In his epistle to the Ephesians, Paul gives a very interesting instruction: *"… Do not get drunk with the wine, for that is dissipation, but be filled with the Spirit."*[102] This reference to drunkenness strikes a bell. Do you remember the accusation of some of the onlookers on the Day of Pentecost as around 120 believers, filled with the Holy Spirit, were speaking with tongues and praising God? They mocked them, saying they were *"full of sweet wine."*[103] Peter then had to stand up and assure the people that these Christians could not be drunk because it was only nine o'clock in the morning. There was nothing in the disciples' behaviour to which Peter could point to disprove the allegation of drunkenness, only the hour of the day?! These Christians *looked* drunk!

They *acted* like drunk people. They were being very vocal, praising God with seemingly reckless abandon. Emotionally and behaviourally, they had lost all inhibition. They appeared to be unconscious of what anyone might think of them, never mind bothered about the consequences. They acted drunk because they *were* drunk, filled with the Holy Spirit! But while we are on the analogy of drunkenness, there is something else worth pointing out.

Drunkenness passes. It is a temporary state, which will eventually wear off. Even the alcoholic cannot stay drunk indefinitely. If he wants to stay under the influence, he must drink more. So it is with the Holy Spirit. The baptism in the Holy Spirit is a wonderful experience, but to remain under His influence we must continually drink and be repeatedly filled.

Back to Paul's instruction to the Ephesians …

---

[102] Ephesians 5:18.
[103] Acts 2:13.

"Do not get drunk with wine," he wrote, "but be filled with the Holy Spirit." In New Testament Greek, the present tense is continuous rather than punctiliar. In other words, Paul is not saying, 'Be filled with the Spirit *as a once-off experience*', but rather, 'Be in an ongoing state of being filled with the Holy Spirit.'

The fullness of the Holy Spirit is the fuel for the road, and the journey is long! We need to continually look outwards towards the vast sea of a lost, broken, hurting, chaotic world to be reminded of our urgent need of being continually filled with the Holy Spirit. The gifts of the Spirit were never intended for workshops or holy huddles, or just for the Christians to bless each other. As soon as the outflow stops, the waters stagnate.

Pentecost is the event that turns the church outwards, boldly and compassionately, to enter a sometimes intimidating, always needy, world. God loves us and so desires to bless us, but the keynote Scripture of evangelicalism, John 3:16, declares that it was for the world – *'kosmos'* – that He sent Jesus. And we, the church, are His chosen instrument in reaching the ends of the earth. What began on the Day of Pentecost will not be completed until all peoples are reached, and Jesus returns to gather His harvest.

> *Lord, may Your kingdom be preached through our lips, demonstrated through our lives, in the power of Your Holy Spirit. Come upon Your people today in power, that through us Jesus might save, heal and deliver. Take our hearts and our minds and our wills. Take our tongues and our hands and our feet. Take our relationships and our livelihoods and our ambitions. Take all of us that there is to have. Touch us again that we might be Your touch to a torn and broken, hurting and dysfunctional, sinful and rebellious world. Yours will be the kingdom. Yours will be the power. Yours will the glory. Amen.*

Printed in Great Britain
by Amazon